My Wars

B-17's to F-4's
WWII to Viet Nam

With Speeds
0 to Mach 2.1

Richard B. Bushong
Colonel USAF
Retired

Table of Contents

CHAPTER 1
My Wars Begin

When the bombing of Pearl Harbor occurred (December 7, 1941), I was working at Wright Field in Dayton Ohio. I had probably the lowest GS (Government Service) rating that was in existence, but I had a "Secret" clearance. My job was to deliver and pick up classified documents from offices of the Staff of Headquarters, Air Service Command. Air Service Command was responsible for the testing and procurement of all air weapons and equipment for the Army Air Force. I was very fortunate to be assigned the job that I had, because I became acquainted with the staff officers and their secretaries and their aides. These acquaintances proved to be very valuable later. The chief of each staff position was a full colonel at the time I worked there.

After the war started, one of the aides (a captain with pilot's wings) kept talking to me about taking the Aviation Cadet exams. He knew that I was very interested in airplanes. On nice days, I took my lunch down to the flight line and watched the aircraft coming and going while I ate my lunch, and he was aware of that. To get into the Aviation Cadet program required 2 years of college or the passing of an equivalency test. I finally decided that he was right and I talked my parents into signing permission for me to take the test and get into the cadet program, if I passed. I passed the test. Twenty-four young men took the test and four passed on the day that I took it. I was elated!

The next day I took the physical exam and passed that, so I thought I was on my way to becoming a pilot. I was told to go back to work and they would notify me when to come back. It was several weeks before I was notified to report back over to Patterson Field, nearby, and be sworn in. The date of my enlistment was April 23, 1942, and I was sworn in as a private in the US Army Air Force. I was told that I was on leave until they called me for appointment as cadet. I could hardly wait.

I went back over to Wright Field and told everyone that I

was now in the Army and awaiting appointment as Aviation Cadet. My supervisor told me that I would have to quit my job because I could not draw two government paychecks at the same time. Since I was a private in the Army and on leave, I was drawing pay for that. The pay for a private at that time was $21 per month, so there I was drawing all that big money (a little sarcasm) and out of a job.

I moved out of my rented room in Dayton and moved back in with my parents in St. Marys, Ohio. It didn't take much moving to get me there, just my clothes. I just loafed around for a couple of weeks and then I could not stand any more of that so I went over to the paper mill where Dad worked and asked for a temporary job. I got one right away, hauling bales of scrap paper into the beater room for the men who worked there to put into the big beaters where it was turned into pulp. Getting a job there was easy since Dad was the beater room foreman and the general manager of the mill was the father of one of my best school chums. I think the pay was about 60 cents per hour, but that was fine for those days. I thought I would be called any day for entry into the Cadet program. As it turned out, it was several months before I was called to active duty and appointed as Aviation Cadet.

In the meantime, the local draft board sent me a notice to come down and register for the draft. I went to the board (living in a small town, I knew all of the board members) and told them that I was already in the army. That was hard for them to believe, since there I was, living at home and standing in front of them in civilian clothes. I showed them my leave orders and it still took a lot of talking to convince the board that I actually was in the army and that they could not draft me. The army had not issued me any uniforms, so I could really understand their suspicions.

I was finally notified to report for duty to Patterson Field on September 1, 1942. I was discharged as a private and appointed "Aviation Cadet". I had been afraid that the war would be over before I was called. As it turned out there was a lot of war left for me. I was sent to Nashville Tennessee to the Aviation

Cadet Classification Center. That was the spot where they decided whether you were to be sent to pilot, bombardier or navigator training. I wanted to be a pilot, but I would have gone to either bombardier or navigator training rather than go into the infantry or go to gunnery school.

We had been issued a couple of sets of fatigues, but no other uniforms. Of course, we had all been run through the barbershop to be shorn. As we marched to the barbershop, all of the guys who had been there a while were yelling "You'll be sorry." and when we got into the barbershop, we knew what they meant. They really whacked it all off.

There were many tests given to us there during the process of deciding whether we were to be sent to pilot, bombardier or navigator school. I sweated out all of those tests and finally the classification lists came out. I was not on any of them. I wondered what had happened to me. All of the guys in my barracks shipped out to schools and there I was just waiting. I started checking to see where the problem was and I found that my physical had been stuck in a drawer and left there. I had been called for a recheck on one part of the eye exam and the medic who did the check just stuck my records into a drawer and forgot about them. My classification proceeded after I found my physical and got it back into the place where it should have been. I came out on the list for pilot school, but I had missed one class. Missing that class just may have been enough to save my life. I will never know.

During the time, I was waiting around, my Mom and Dad drove down from Ohio. We had not been issued any uniforms yet, except for the fatigues, and I could not go to town in those, so I went over to the BX and bought a uniform. I got permission to go into town and see my parents, so there I was, only on active duty for a few weeks and walking around in Nashville with my parents. The Cadet uniform and visor cap looked somewhat like an officer's uniform; so many of the army personnel walking the streets of Nashville were saluting me. I casually returned all of the salutes and my folks thought I was already a big shot. My head swelled so big I could hardly keep my cap on. I was nineteen years old at that time.

Finally, I was given orders to report to Kelly Field in San Antonio, Texas. I was being sent to another classification center to await an opening in a pilot training class. Since I had already been classified as a pilot trainee I did not have to go through the classification process again. I just had to wait around for a class opening. I was not alone; all of the guys in my barracks at Kelly Field were waiting. They, however, had been classified right there, while I had been classified in Nashville.

CHAPTER 2
Preflight

The great day arrived. We were assigned to Class 43G and sent to Preflight right there at Kelly Field. Each of the four sections of our pilot training was to last for 10 weeks. They were designated: Preflight, Primary Flight Training, Basic Flight Training and Advanced Flight Training. From our lowly position as Underclassmen in Preflight, it looked like an impossible chore ahead of us. The Upperclassmen were kings and we were the peasants. We were hazed unmercifully by the Upperclassmen. It was especially easy for them to pick on us at mealtime. We had to sit on the first 4 inches of our chair and sit at attention while eating a "square meal". A "square meal" consisted of taking food onto your fork, then straight up to a point even with your mouth and then a 90-degree turn to your mouth. There were numerous other interferences with our meals, such as; an Upperclassman would ask a cadet what he was famous for and the Underclassman would have to get up, stand on his chair and tell the whole mess hall what he was famous for. I was famous for sawing toilet seats in half. When asked why I did that, I replied, "For half-assed upperclassmen". They laughed and I got by with it. The requests and the replies were all silly things, but what we did there was one method of teaching us discipline. The upperclassmen had complete authority over us and the officers in charge of each squadron were like God. The only thing that we had to look forward to was that in 5 weeks we would become the Upperclassmen.

We rose early and had a full day of training. We did a lot of marching with each of us having to be a squad leader, at times, and march the troops, so we were learning to command as well as obey commands. We had a very strenuous Physical Training (PT) program and many ground school classes. We studied

Aeronautics, Morse code, Aircraft Identification (both friends and foes), Meteorology, Customs of the Service, The Geneva Convention and The Articles of War. They really kept us busy. We also pulled guard duty a few times during our time as Underclassmen.

One night, after "lights out", we were all lying there trying to get to sleep, when one of the guys in an upper bunk said in a very loud voice, "Has anyone been trying to read the message that cricket is sending?" We had been studying Morse code so much that he was reading a message from the cricket's chirping. We all got a big laugh out of that and then everyone listened to the cricket's chirping and tried to read his message. I never did figure out what message he was sending, but then, I never was very good with Morse code anyhow. We had to be able to read 20 words per minute and send 15 words per minute. We all became somewhat proficient, but that cricket had never attended our class.

While I was in Preflight, the legendary General Hap Arnold, Chief of the Army Air Force, visited Kelly to address the Aviation Cadets. There was a huge formation of all of the cadets on the massive parade ground. We stood at attention for so long that numerous Cadets passed out. They were carried off the parade ground on stretchers to the waiting ambulances. It was expected that some would pass out.

After we became Upperclassmen, we were permitted to go into town on pass, so we got to see San Antonio. On one pass a couple of buddies and I went into a nice restaurant down by the river and had a steak dinner. I had never seen a steak like that in my young life. It was huge. It hung over the platter and was about ¾ of an inch thick. Where I grew up that would have been a meal for the whole family. I ate the whole thing.

CHAPTER 3
Primary Flight Training

When Preflight finally ended, we were sent to Primary Flight School. My assignment was to Brady, Texas, a small town at the geographic heart of Texas. Our class (43G) was spread out among many places for Primary. All of the Primary Flight Training fields for us were in Texas, since we were in the Gulf Coast Training Command. At Brady, our flight instructors were all civilians. The check pilots were Army Air Force officers, Lieutenants and Captains. As I remember, the Commandant of the school was a Major. In Primary, the "wash-out" rate was horrendous. Forty to fifty percent of the Cadets were "washed out" (eliminated from cadet training). Most of the washouts were from inability to handle the aircraft, but some were for physical reasons. Some of the cadets became airsick every time they went up and could not overcome the problem. We were all afraid of washing out, because we were in the Army, and washouts were sent to other branches of the Army, many to the Infantry. We certainly did not want that. We were all GUNG-HO to become pilots, but for many, it was not to be.

Shortly after we got there, the Commandant asked if any of the cadets played either drum or bugle. He wanted to have a drum and bugle corps so he could have music to accompany the parades he had scheduled. I had played the drum in the high school marching band for years and had several good marching rhythms, so I was selected as the head drummer. There were three other guys who had played drums and about eight buglers. We got together in the evenings, practiced, and actually got pretty good. Being in the Drum and Bugle Corps may have kept several of us from washing out (who knows?). We played for several parades there in Primary. It was kind of fun.

We were assigned to our barracks by alphabetical order, so I was in with the A's, B's and C's. My bunkmate (upper) was

Bob Cordell. In the next bunk set was Sam Crosby, a good old Texas boy. Bob, Sam and I became close friends. We studied together and partied together. When we were able to get passes to go to town, we three always stayed together. We did some drinking, although none of us was 21, no one even questioned us when we bought a drink. We were soldiers and in uniform all the time, so no questions were asked about our age.

Sam was really funny when he had a couple of drinks. He stuttered. He didn't just stutter the first letter of a word; he stuttered whole words. He would say something like, "Can,can,can we,we,we go,go,go back to,to,to the base,base,base now?" We all got a kick out of Sam's stutter and we got to calling him Sam, Sam, Sam. Everyone in our barracks got a laugh at Sam's stuttering. He didn't do it when he was sober. I later (much later) ran into Sam again. He was stationed at Headquarters. Tactical Air Command, at Langley AFB in Virginia and I was stationed at Headquarters. Special Operations Forces, at Eglin AFB in Florida. I went up to TAC Headquarters on temporary assignment and I walked into Sam's office to see if it was the Sam Crosby that I had been buddies with back in Primary Flight School in 1942. I had spotted his name on some correspondence that we had received in Florida. It was the same Sam. We were both full Colonels when we met again and both had been through a couple of wars. It was a nice reunion and we had quite a long talk.

The aircraft that we had for our Primary Training was the PT-19. It was a low wing monoplane with two open cockpits. The wing was made of plywood and therefore the plane was tagged with the nickname of "Bamboo Bomber". It was a pretty good airplane and very forgiving of all the mistakes that we made. It had no radio equipment. The control tower controlled us with different colored lights from a light gun. It was easy to see why no one could become a pilot who was colorblind. Our instructor pilot talked to us through a "Goss port" which was two rubber tubes (about like the tubes of a stethoscope) connected to our helmet. His voice came to us through the rubber tubes. It was purely a one-way conversation.

Our flight program for Primary was about 60 hours of flying. Part of the flying was with an instructor and part was solo. We were supposed to solo at about eight hours of flying time. That was a big day for us. If we made it that far and soloed, we were wet-down when we finished. All of our buddies would be waiting and would forcibly escort us to the shower and we were dunked, flight suit and all. Of course, we were so thrilled to have soloed that we did not mind the dunking. That was the point where many washouts occurred. If the instructor pilot did not feel that the cadet was capable of soloing he was eliminated from the program. There was no profit in spending more time on him, so he then became a private in the Army and was assigned elsewhere in ground forces. For us that would be a terrible fate. Luckily, that did not happen to me.

I did have a few very interesting happenings during Primary. After I had about four or five hours in the PT-19, my instructor showed me a spin. He pulled the aircraft into a stall and kicked right rudder and away we went, nose down, spinning. He was talking to me all during the maneuver, telling me what he was doing. He let the aircraft do two full turns and then kicked opposite rudder and popped the stick forward, stopping the spin and getting the aircraft out of the stalled condition. He then applied power and smoothly pulled the nose back up to the level position. He asked me if I understood the entry into a spin and the recovery procedure. I nodded yes; our conversation in the PT-19 was one way only, him to me. He said, "OK, you do a 2 turn spin and recover". I pulled the aircraft into a stall, kicked and held the right rudder and away we went, spinning, nose down. At the 2 turn spot, (as nearly as I could tell) I kicked the opposite rudder and popped the stick forward. The only difference between what he did and what I did was that I *held* the stick forward instead of bringing it back to neutral after I popped it. The aircraft recovered from the spin OK, but what I was doing forced the nose of the plane to go back beyond straight down so that we were actually doing a part of an outside loop (not good). I realized that we should not be going way back under like that, so I pulled back on the stick really hard, so hard that I blacked-out the instructor and myself. Nothing was very serious; we recovered our vision as soon as I relaxed the hard pull in the stick. He very carefully explained what I had done wrong and got a chuckle out of it. Instructing kids who had never flown before must have been a tough job.

During Primary, we also receive training in the "Link Trainer" This was a device for teaching us to fly on instruments without any visual reference to the outside world. It was like the cockpit of an airplane, we got inside, and the instructor pulled the hood over us so we could not see outside at all. We then "flew" the machine in all kinds of instrument conditions. The Link did not leave the ground, but we could make it turn, dive, climb and do all sorts of maneuvers while safely operating inside the Link Trainer building. Of course, we were just learning the basics of instrument flying while at Primary, but the Link Trainer was used for years to train us on instrument flying. The Link went out of service years later when the sophisticated simulators were developed for each type of aircraft.

When we were near graduation from Primary, my Mom took a train all the way from Ohio to Brady Texas to see her little boy. I was glad to see her and, aside from being restricted to the base to walk penalty tours for one evening, we had a nice visit. We had to get a few more flying hours and the weather was not cooperating, so the commandant decided to send us out with low ceilings. I guess the ceiling was about 1000 feet. Off we went. I flew over to the motel where Mom was staying and buzzed it a couple of times. I saw someone come out of the office and was afraid that they would get my aircraft number and report me for buzzing. That could be a washout offence. I pulled up into the low clouds and was completely on instruments. After I zoomed up into the clouds, I kept climbing, I thought. My instrument skills were at a bare minimum, so I was very confused. I remembered what they had pounded into my head in the Link Trainer "needle, ball and airspeed" and discovered that I was indeed in a spiral, going down at a rapid rate. I was able to right the aircraft and begin a gradual descent until I broke out of the cloud deck. It was a good thing that there were no hills around Brady. Needless to say, I was really scared and did not do that again. We got our required hours (about 60) and graduated from Primary and onward and upward to Basic Flight Training.

Cocky Pilot
Primary Flight Training
Note ports on side of Helmet for rubber tubes

CHAPTER 4
Basic Flight Training

Basic Flight Training was at Goodfellow Field at San Angelo, Texas. There were cadets from several Primary training fields assigned to class 43G at Goodfellow. After we all got there, we were assigned to squadrons. The way we were assigned was by size. All the cadets were assembled and we were told that if we were taller than the guy ahead of us was we were to move forward. This went on until we had four squadrons of cadets, each squadron being pretty nearly the same size. This made the squadrons look a lot better when marching, but there was another reason for sizing. Many of the shorter cadets were sent to single engine Advanced Training after finishing Basic. Many of the smaller guys became fighter pilots and the bigger guys were sent to twin engine Advanced Training and then to bombers or cargo planes. The cockpits in the single engine fighter aircraft were not as roomy as the cockpits in the larger aircraft.

We called the guys in the shortest squadron "pillow pilots", because the seats in the BT-13 were not adjustable up and down, and when they went out to fly they would have a couple of pillows under their arms to put in the seat to get them high enough to see over the instrument panel.

The BT-13 was nicknamed the "Vultee Vibrator" because it was made by Vultee and it did vibrate. It was a more powerful aircraft than the PT-19 that we had in Primary and it had a canopy that closed over the two seats. It also had a radio and an intercom for two-way communication between the student and instructor. The landing gear was fixed (not retractable). It also had a two-speed prop, high pitch for cruise and low pitch for take-off and climb. We also put the prop into the low pitch position for landing in case we had to go around.

The instructor that I was assigned to was a 1st Lieutenant and we did not get along too well. I tried hard to please him, but could not seem to get anything just the way he wanted it. After about 5 hours with him, he put me up for a check ride. The Check Pilot was a Captain and a tough one to please. We had heard about how rough he was and we were all very apprehensive. There were five of us scheduled for a check ride that day, all with the same Check Pilot. We all sat on a bench with our parachutes and waited until he called for us by name. He had flown with the first three when he got to me. As I remember, two of the first three did not pass their check ride and were washed out. We could tell, as each one got out of the airplane and walked toward us, how they had done. One was elated and two were downcast, almost crying.

He called for me and I was shaking in my boots. I just knew he was going to wash me out. The only reason we had been put up for a check ride at this point was that our instructor did not think we were going to make it. The Check Pilot got into the rear cockpit and I got into the front one. He told me what he wanted me to do, get clearance, take off and climb to 5000 feet. When we got there, he had me do a series of maneuvers, stalls, spins, snap rolls, slow rolls, loops, Immelman rolls and I just did everything perfectly. He said, "OK land the aircraft." We were miles from Goodfellow Field, so I looked around and could not see anywhere that looked like a landing field. He pointed to a small auxiliary landing field that I had not seen. It was just a farm field that had a wind T in the middle of it so we could tell which way the wind was blowing. I did a traffic pattern and landed. He told me to go around and do another one. I did, both were good landings. He told me to stop the aircraft at the middle of the field and he got out on the wing and leaned into my cockpit and said, "Are you ready to solo?" I promptly said, "Yes Sir!" and he said, "No you're not, your radio is still on intercom and you have to have it on radio when you are alone in the aircraft." That scared the hell out of me. I thought he was going to wash me out right there. I switched my radio to the proper position and he told me to go ahead and solo and make a couple of landings. He watched me from beside the wind T. He waved me over and he got in and told me to take us back to Goodfellow. By then, I did not even know where Goodfellow was. He laughed about that and told me which direction to go to get home. I landed and taxied to our squadron area and shut the aircraft down and got out. I was so elated that I felt like I was still flying. I was walking about 3 feet off the ground. I had soloed on a check-ride.

I was assigned to a new instructor and we got along fine. He was a frustrated fighter pilot. He wanted to be fighting the war instead of instructing cadets. He was an excellent pilot and I learned a lot from him. There were times when he would try to make that old BT-13 into a fighter. He would dive, maneuver, take his hand mike, and tap the switch on his leg and in our headsets; it would make a "Ta-Ta-Ta-Ta-Ta-Ta" sound, like a machine gun. If there had been enemy fighters over Texas, he would have shot down bunches of them. He was excellent at aerobatics and loved doing them, so I got proficient at all of the maneuvers.

One day, after I had been flying with him for about a week, I was letting down to enter the down-wind leg of the traffic pattern and he took the controls. We were at 1500 feet and he rolled the aircraft over and did the neatest roll. We stayed right in the seat during the entire maneuver. I had never done anything like that and I thought it was great. As he rolled out to level flight, he was at a perfect 1000 feet and was into the traffic pattern for landing. I asked him what that roll was and he said, "That was a barrel roll." I landed and taxied in and he got out and told me to go up for an hour and practice what we had been doing on the flight. The things we were doing were all maneuvers at about 5000 feet and were aerobatics. I did my hour of practice and came back to Goodfellow. As I approached the entry into the traffic pattern, I was at 1500 feet and I rolled the aircraft over, attempting to do a barrel roll like my instructor had done earlier. I had never done the maneuver and he had not explained it to me when he had done it, but I thought it was so neat when he did it that I would do it just like he did. The only problem was, I didn't know how to do the maneuver. I got upside down and then started toward the ground. I did what they called a "split S" which is the bottom half of the S. I was headed toward the ground and was not very high. I pulled back on the stick as hard as I could and pulled the aircraft out of the dive, but I was down in a creek-bed. There were mesquite trees on the sides of the creek that were higher than I was. I scared myself nearly to death. The interesting part of the story is that I never tried a barrel roll again until I was flying a single engine jet aircraft in Japan, nearly 20 years later. The maneuver was very easy to do.

Chapter 5
Advanced Flight Training

When we finished Basic, we were sent to Advanced Flight Training. That is generally where the "Pillow Pilots" were separated from the taller guys. I think most of the taller ones went to Twin-engine Advanced. I was sent to Ellington Field, near Houston. Our aircraft for our advanced training were the AT-9 and AT-10. They were both twin-engine aircraft.

We did a lot of cross-country flying, practice engine failure and instrument flying. Our ground school was more advanced sessions of the same things that we had been studying since Preflight. Some of our cross-country flying was done at night.

The aircraft that we flew were primitive, when compared to today's aircraft, but they were sophisticated to us. They had side-by-side seating in the cockpit, so we were getting used to the pilot-co-pilot arrangement and duties. They also had retractable landing gear. We flew with instructors for the first few flights and then it was usually two cadets on the flights.

Houston is situated on the Gulf of Mexico and since we were there in the summer months (June and July); it was common for us to have towering cumulus clouds form in the afternoons. We used to go into the cloud formations and fly into the tunnels and openings in the clouds. We had a lot of fun climbing and diving through the cloud formations. We were cocky pilots by then. We also got frequent showers and sometimes they were very heavy. We occasionally were sent to the municipal airport to land and wait out the storms.

We were granted a lot more freedom, since we were pretty close to being commissioned as officers in the Army Air Force. We were allowed to go to town and around to other towns on weekends. One of my flying buddies and I went to Galveston one weekend and there was a big amusement park there. He and I went on the roller coaster and he was scared to death. I got the biggest kick out of his fear on the roller coaster, because he did not show any fear during all kinds of maneuvers in an aircraft.

We were also fitted for our officer uniforms. We were to be given a $250.00 allowance when we were commissioned, to purchase our uniforms and the merchants that were selling the uniforms were pretty sure that we were going to graduate so they measured, fitted and tailored the uniforms in advance. I spent slightly more than the $250.00 allowance for my uniforms. They had to have them ready for our graduation, because we had to turn in our cadet issued clothing and be ready to transfer immediately after graduation.

Graduation was to be a great day and we were really looking forward to getting our wings and second Lieutenant's bars. The graduation was to be held in the base theater, but nature interfered. A couple of days before graduation a hurricane hit Houston. I do not know if they named them in those days or not, but that one was a DANDY. The winds on the front side were 135 MPH when they hit our base. Someone decided that the aircraft would survive the storm better if there were a couple of cadets hanging onto the tie-down ropes on each wing of the aircraft, so we were out in the storm, hanging onto those ropes. It must have worked, because we only lost a couple of aircraft and only a few cadets were injured.

The eye of the storm went directly over us. The winds were calm and the sky was blue overhead. It took quite a few minutes for the eye to pass over us and then the winds came from the opposite direction. We had turned the aircraft during the time the eye was over us so that they would be facing into the new wind direction for the backside of the hurricane. The winds on the backside were 123 MPH, just a breeze after the front side.

The base suffered pretty badly from the storm. The roof was blown off nearly every building on the base. The base theater was de-roofed and all wet inside, so our graduation was moved to the ramp in front of one of the hangers. It worked for me. I did not care where it took place as long as I got those wings and bars.

Two guys in our class were held back for one class. They had come back to the base a few days before graduation was scheduled and the bottom of their aircraft had rice plants plastered to it. The powers-that-be decided that they might have been buzzing at a very low altitude and punished them by holding them back one class. (By a rare coincidence, one of them was the brother of my future wife's aunt. I didn't even know my wife to-be at that time.)

It had been explained to us that it was an old custom of the army that the first enlisted man who saluted us after we pinned on the wings and bars was to be rewarded with a dollar. I am sure that there were several GI's who had done this before and found it quite profitable, because there were several standing on the road back to our barracks area and saluting everyone in sight. They picked up a pile of $1 bills that day. I was sure glad to give my dollar to someone. We were all so proud of our wings and bars.

A new rank was just introduced about the time of our graduation. It was Flight Officer and the ones who received that rank were not commissioned officers. They were equivalent to a warrant officer. There were four in our class. I do not know how they were selected.

Chapter 6
B-17 Training

We were all given a delay enroute to our next duty station, our first duty as officers. I went home to St. Marys, Ohio to show off my new wings and bars. I was so proud, strutting around town. I was pleased with my next assignment. I was assigned to B-17 Combat Crew Phase Training. I was particularly fond of the B-17, "The Flying Fortress" and I had put that as my preferred aircraft for my assignment after graduation. My delay enroute, which counted as leave, was for a couple of weeks and then I was to report to Ephrata, Washington. That was also exciting for me as I had never been that far west. I traveled from Houston, Texas to St. Marys, Ohio and then to Ephrata, Washington all by train. It was a long slow trip.

When I arrived at Ephrata, I was astounded. The base consisted of a bunch of tarpaper shacks for living quarters. Everyone was assigned to a flight crew. There were gunners, radio operators, flight engineers, navigators, bombardiers and pilots. The crews were formed arbitrarily and then, if there were any incompatibilities, the people were moved about until the crews were stabilized. Each crew consisted of four gunners, one radio operator, one flight engineer, one navigator, one bombardier and two pilots. All crewmembers received some gunnery training during our combat crew training, so we could all operate the guns if needed, but all of the enlisted personnel had attended gunnery school. The 1st pilot had gone to B-17 Transition Training straight from pilot school, so he had been specially trained for a couple of months on the B-17. Generally, the ones selected for that training were a few years older than the average cadet. Gill, who was our crew commander, was 25 (an old man); I was 20 at that time. I was co-pilot on the crew.

After our crew was selected, we started our training and started getting acquainted with each other. We had ground school, gunnery training, skeet shooting (to teach us how to lead the fighter aircraft that were going to be shooting at us), aircraft identification, aircraft systems study (for pilots and flight engineers) and flight training. In our flight-training phase, we had all sorts of missions to fly. We did some gunnery missions out over the ocean with towed targets to shoot at. We had various navigational missions, bombing missions, practice formation flying, and night missions. A lot of the flying was to get us to operate as a team and we began to count on each other to do our various chores. It worked. We became more familiar with the aircraft each day and became a close-knit operating crew.

We had only been at Ephrata for a short time, I was walking down a dusty road between the tarpaper shacks and an enlisted man coming toward me saluted, and I recognized him from my previous life. When I was working at Wright Field in Dayton, I had rented a room in a private house. The man I had just met was the son of my landlady back in Dayton. We stopped and had a talk about what had happened to us in the year and a half since I had seen him. He and I had some good chess sessions while I lived in his Mom's house. I don't think I ever saw him again

After a few weeks at Ephrata, we were moved to Walla Walla to continue our training. About 2 1/2 months, total, of intensive training and we were ready to go fight someone. We did not know which direction we would be going to do our fighting. The war was intense in either direction.

During the time we were at Walla Walla, a few of us went into town to see a movie. As we were sitting in the theater, waiting for the movie to start, I felt a tap on my shoulder. I turned around and there was Don Miller, a kid from my high school class in St. Marys, Ohio. He was in a Navy organization that was taking college training there in Walla Walla. We chatted for a time and I arranged for him to come out to the base to see the beautiful airplane that I was privileged to get to fly. We had a good visit. I didn't see Don again for a good many years.

We had been formed into a Composite Bomb Group

during our training, and we shipped out as a group. There were 35 B-17 crews plus a small cadre of headquarters personnel. We boarded a troop train and headed east. Troop trains moved very slowly, or at least ours did. The accommodations were far from deluxe, too. There was a mess car on the train and we were assigned times to go eat. We slept sitting in the seats. There were many card games going on night and day.

We stopped at a base in Kansas and we had to do some more testing and we were issued some new equipment, jackets, Colt .45 automatic pistols, shoulder holsters and some other stuff. It sure looked like someone was getting serious about sending us to war. We still did not know where we were going. They took us out to the flight line, positioned our whole crew in front of a B-17, and took our picture. I do not remember how I got a copy of it but I found it years later.

Gill's Crew - The tall one in back is me

After a few days, we boarded another troop train and headed out again. I don't know if they were trying to confuse the enemy or us but that train took such a roundabout route that we were near New Orleans on our way from Kansas to New Jersey. We finally arrived in Camp Kilmer, New Jersey and we had a few days there. I got to call home, but I could not tell my folks where I was nor where I was headed. I really was not sure where we were headed, but we were pretty sure that we were going somewhere in the European Theater of Operations. After a few days in Camp Kilmer, we were routed out of our barracks at night and boarded a train to the harbor. We then filed on board the ship, carrying all of our luggage. The ship we boarded was the Queen Elizabeth. What a thrill that was for me. I had never been on any water vessel larger than a rowboat.

The Queen Elizabeth had never been used for civilian travel. When it was completed, the war was going on and it was immediately converted to a troop transport. We officers had deluxe accommodations; there were 18 of us crammed into a cabin that was designed for one or two people. There were bunks along the walls, quite close together, and our luggage was stacked in the middle of the cabin. It was a tight fit. We were told that there were 17,000 troops on board that ship. We were also informed that we would be going across the Atlantic unescorted, that the ship could outrun the sub-packs that were all over the Atlantic. They also told us that the ship would change course every three minutes so the subs could not get a good torpedo launch. Apparently, they knew what they were doing, because we got across the Atlantic without being hit by a torpedo.

We were assigned a table in the main dining room and two times a day to be there for meals. It did not make any difference if it was night or day when our times came up to be at the table to eat we had better be there. The food was excellent and the service was good. The room was really packed with tables. I suppose that the areas that were designed for dance floors and entertainment were being used for dining tables.

As I said, we officers were really living in luxury. There was a steward assigned to our area, He took care of several staterooms. He would bring us a pitcher of fresh water for shaving and washing our hands and face. There was a small bathroom adjoining the stateroom and, if we bathed, it was in salt water. You can imagine the quantity of fresh water that would be consumed by 17,000 troops each day. It was an exciting voyage in many ways and very boring in many other ways. We read a lot and played a lot of cards in our stateroom.

The navigator on our crew, Ed Cannon, just about cleaned out all of the cash from the guys in our stateroom. He had quite a bit of money after about three days of poker. He heard about an enlisted man down in the lower part of the ship that had almost cleaned out all of the cash from the troops down there in a continuous crap game. The rumor was that he had twenty to thirty thousand dollars and was taking on all comers in his crap game. Ed decided to go down there and clean him out. He departed our stateroom about 7:00 PM, with all of his winnings, determined to come back with all of that GI's money. He came back about 2:30 the next morning - BROKE. The GI had cleaned him out. We heard that the GI got off the ship with a fortune when we arrived in Europe.

We zigged and zagged our way across the Atlantic and the system for avoiding the U-boats worked as advertised. We landed in Glasgow Scotland. What a pleasant surprise. We got off the Queen Elizabeth and were greeted by numerous volunteer ladies. They certainly did their best to make us feel welcome. I remember one of them giving me a Coke in a bottle, shaped just like the Coke bottles at home and, to my surprise, the Coke tasted just like a Coke in Ohio.

Chapter 7
390th Bomb Group (H)
There are good days to be in the Hospital!

We processed through a replacement depot and the 35 aircrews were assigned to the 390th Bomb Group (H) at Framlingham, England. Framlingham US Army Air Force base was located near the eastern coast of England. There was a Framlingham Castle nearby from which the Base took its name. We were located about 30 miles from the larger city of Ipswich. There was a small village near our base named Parham. The air base was constructed on land that had been farmland and some farming was still being done around the base.

We learned that the Bomb Group had come over from the States in July 1943 and had flown their first mission in August 1943. It was now November 1943. We were to replace crews that had been shot down and crews that had finished their tour and were being shipped home. We also built up the total force of the 390th.

The night that we arrived at the 390^{th,} there was a celebration in the Officer's Club for William Royal and his crew. They had come over to England with the 390th when the Group came over from the States They had finished their 25 missions and were eligible to return to the States. They had been to some pretty rough spots in Germany, such as, Schweinfurt and Marienburg and had survived. There were some remarks going around about "If they can do it, so can we."

We had been told that, if we completed 25 missions we could go home. I asked a question of someone at the club that night, "What is the average loss per mission?" The answer that I got was "About 5% per mission". All that math that I took in high school enabled me to figure that the odds were 125% against a crew being able to finish their required 25 missions. I did not like those odds, but what was a guy to do. We were all anxious to go mb the Germans. We were all young and invincible (I

,oyal was finished flying his combat missions and we got his au, lane, "Royal Flush". We were pleased to get that airplane because it had certainly been lucky for Royal and his crew. The airplane had only flown 23 combat missions; Royal had used other planes, at times, during his 25 missions.

We flew an orientation mission and a practice formation mission just to get us familiar with the area and the way that the 390th liked to fly formation. During our training in the States, we had never flown formation at the altitudes that the missions were to be flown, nor had we flown the aircraft at the weights we were to carry into combat. Our practice missions there in England were not at those altitudes and weights either, so nothing in our training had prepared us for our actual flight conditions in combat.

We had only been at Framlingham for about a week when I got very sick one night. I started vomiting and really felt bad. I went over to the Flight Surgeon's office and he checked me over and said, "I'm going to keep you here in the clinic tonight and tomorrow you are going to the hospital." The next day I was taken to the hospital by ambulance. The hospital was located about 30 miles from our base. I was diagnosed as having "Yellow Jaundice", called Hepatitis today. I was put into a ward with several other guys who had already turned yellow. I was very sick for a while, but I did not turn as yellow as some of the guys in the same ward.

After I was in the hospital for a few days, and was feeling a little better, a couple of enlisted men from our crew came over to see me. It was not easy to get over there because of the distance and the lack of transportation. They had hitch-hiked over. I was glad to see them since I kind of felt like an orphan child, away from everybody that I knew. We visited for a while and then they had to get back to the base. Daylight hours were short in England in December and they had to catch a ride to get back to Framlingham. After that visit, no more of my crew came over to see me. I figured that they must be very busy back at the 390th and I knew that it was difficult to get over to the hospital so I was not too concerned.

I finally was released from the hospital. It was Christmas Eve 1943. I, too, had to hitch a ride back to the base. I rode back in an ambulance that was going my way. When I got to the base, I walked over to the 569th Squadron area and went to the Quonset hut that we had been assigned. There had been 12 officers in that hut, including me. Each crew had four officers, two Pilots, a Navigator and a Bombardier, so in that hut was the officer complement of three crews. We had all come in together and had trained together in the States. I opened the door to the hut and turned on the lights and eleven of the twelve mattresses were rolled up. My bed was still made. My clothes were still hanging, but all others were gone.

I went over to the orderly room and asked the CQ (charge of quarters) where my crew had been moved. I told him which hut they had been in and the name of the pilot (Gill). He said, "You had better go over to the hut next door and talk to Major Pennibaker, the Squadron Operations Officer." I went over to Major Pennibaker's hut and knocked. He told me to come in. I told him who I was and asked where my crew was. He said, "Oh, they were shot down. All three crews that were in your hut were shot down."

You can imagine my shock. I know that I turned pale. I felt like someone had hit me in the solar plexus. Major Pennibaker saw how his news affected me and told me to sit down. He poured me a big slug of Bourbon and told me that he did not want me going back over to that hut to sleep. He had an extra bunk in his hut and he told me that I could sleep there that night. I was greatly relieved that I did not have to go back over to that hut and sleep there alone with the eleven rolled-up bunks. I did not know if my crewmembers were dead or prisoners at that time. I later found out that the report of the shoot-down said that there were 10 parachutes spotted coming out of the plane when it went down. The plane, the "Royal Flush" was shot down by fighters over Bremen, Germany on the 16th of December 1944. It was my crew's first mission.

Chapter 8
New Crew - Start Combat

The next day I was assigned to Norman (Bud) Palmer's crew as co-pilot. Their co-pilot had taken my place on the day that Gill's crew was shot down. The guy who took my place was named Embree and I have, many times since then, jokingly blamed him for my crew being shot down. My rationale for blaming him was:

1. He had only flown one combat mission before he flew with my crew and they ran out of gas on that mission and had to ditch the airplane in the North Sea. One of the crew died due to exposure to the cold water of the North Sea. The rest were rescued.

2. He then flew as a substitute for me with my crew and they were shot down.

It seems to me that he was a bad luck type of person; he only flew two combat missions and never made it home on either occasion.

I have since obtained a copy of the flight order for Gill's crew for the day that they were shot down and there were ten names typed on the order, mine included, and my name was crossed off and Embree's name was inserted in pencil. That was a good day to be in the hospital! My crewmembers were all captured and in Stalag Luft for about 20 months. It was too bad that they did not have old Lucky (me) along.

Well, my new assignment was to Palmer's crew to replace Embree. As you can imagine, I was not welcomed with open arms. I think that they kind of blamed me for fact that Embree was missing in action. It was not very long before I was accepted as a member of the crew. We flew one practice mission around England to get me back into the feel of flying formation. I also had some time in the Link Trainer (instrument trainer). We flew

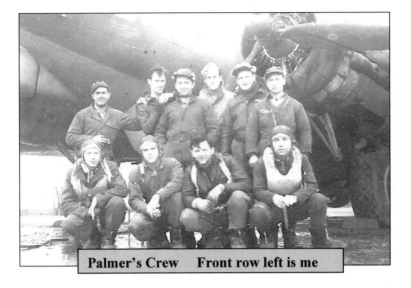

Palmer's Crew   Front row left is me

our first combat mission together on the 30th of December 1943. It was to Ludwigshaven, Germany. Our target was a chemical plant. It was my first mission, but the rest of the crew had flown several by then.

I was anxious to go. I wanted to see the whole thing, the FLAK, the fighters and all of the action. I saw a lot of it that first day. It was exciting. There was a lot of Flak over the target and, at one time, the Group was attacked by a wave of 20 FW-190's and one of our aircraft was shot down by the fighters. So, I had my first mission under my belt. I was now a combat veteran. The total flight time for my first mission was 8 hours and 15 minutes.

I flew another practice mission and did some more instrument training in the Link trainer and it was eight days later that we flew combat again, and guess where we went, Ludwigshaven again. We were after the same target and on both occasions, we bombed through the clouds using a pathfinder aircraft as the lead aircraft. The pathfinder aircraft had radar installed and, although it was primitive, it allowed us to do a fairly good job of bombing with complete cloud cover. The intelligence report on that mission said that the results were good.

On that second mission, there was little fighter activity and the Flak was less intense over the target. The first group over the target was hit harder than we were. The total flight time on my second mission was 6 hours and 30 minutes. The difference in the flight time for the two missions to Ludwigshaven was because we took a shorter route to the target on the second mission.

Now I had two missions under my belt and I felt like a seasoned veteran even though I was still a green kid. I had had some practice at flying a tight formation at high altitude and felt as if I was doing a pretty good job of it. Those first two missions were flown over cloud cover and fighter activity was not intense.

The temperatures were always extreme at the altitudes that we flew. It was common to see -30 or -40 on our outside air temperature gage. We had a little heat in the cockpit. It came from our #2 engine manifold and was blown across our windshield to defrost it, but it did provide a little warm air in the cockpit. We did not wear the same clothing that the five men in the back of the aircraft wore. There was no heat back there and if it was 40 below outside, it was 40 below inside. The crew back there wore the electric suit and the sheepskins over it. The electric suit plugged into the aircraft electrical system. The F model had open waist windows and that created a little more breeze back there. The G model had Plexiglas in the waist windows with the gun mounted through it.

My third mission, January 11, 1944, was to Brunswick. The target was an aircraft engine factory where many of the engines for the ME-110's, FW-190's and the JU-88's were manufactured. All-out attempts were being made to eliminate the Luftwaffe in two ways; shoot them out of the skies and bomb their factories to stop production of new aircraft. As we proceeded deeper into Germany, the weather in England was deteriorating and a recall signal was sent. Many of the bomber forces, including us, did not receive the recall order and proceeded onward to their targets. Unfortunately, many of the fighter escort groups got the recall signal and returned to England. Only 152 heavy bombers proceeded to the target

The Germans put up the largest interceptor force since 14 October 1943 on the Schweinfurt raid when 60 heavy bombers were lost. The 8th Air Force again lost 60 heavy bombers on this raid. The Germans claimed, in their news releases, that 124 heavy bombers were shot down. They anticipated that we were going to send part of the heavy bombers to Berlin on this raid so they did everything that they could do to stop us. I made this note in the little diary that I kept; "We had to fly in another group formation which broke up when we climbed through some clouds. We went over Germany to the target with only 14 ships in the formation. Luckily, we were not picked on by fighters-----60 ships shot down. Lucky to still be alive." The loss that day was nearly 40% of the bombers that went to the target.

After surviving that one, I really felt like a seasoned veteran. Wow, I only had 22 more to go to get to that magic 25 missions.

We went to the Officers' Club every evening. The Officers' Mess (dining room) was in the same building, so we went there to eat even if we were scheduled to fly the next day and could not have a drink. One evening, when the Group was on a "stand-down" and we would not have to fly the next day, we were having a few drinks in the O-Club bar. A young 2nd Lt. climbed up on one of the tables and began to sing in a beautiful tenor voice. The whole bar quieted down while he sang the following song:

"Oh, it was late in the evening,
The gang was all leaving.
O'Reilly was closing the bar,
When he turned round and said
To the lady in red
Get out - you can't stay where you are.

31

Oh, she wept a big tear in her bucket of beer,
As she thought of the cold night ahead.
Then a gentleman dapper stepped out of the crapper
And these are the words that he said,

'Her mother never told her
The things that a young girl should know
Of their foibles and their fancies
And the way men come and go.
You have stolen her youth and her beauty
And time has left its scar
So remember your sisters and mothers, boys
And let her sleep under the bar."

Every one in the bar applauded loudly and asked him to sing it again and again. It became a routine for him to jump up on a table and start singing the song and, after a few times, we all knew the words and joined in singing at the top of our voices along with the real singer.

A few days later we flew a practice mission. We had to keep that formation flying really tight. We briefed on three missions, the 18th, 19th, and 20th of January and got everything ready to go and then the missions were scrubbed due to bad weather over the target areas. There was a lot of effort went into getting ready for a mission, we were up early and briefed and prepared the aircraft to go, so we had put in a lot of work by the time it was scrubbed. We were all ready to go and out at the aircraft waiting and then we would see a red flare shot into the air from the control tower scrubbing the mission. The tension had been building while we were waiting. It was always a relief when we saw that red flare, but a real let down, too, because we were ready to go and then had to undo all of our effort.

We finally got off on a mission on the 21st of January. It was a short mission, four hours flight time, and we bombed a rocket installation in Heuringham, France. We called it a milk run (easy mission). The Flak over the target was intense and accurate, but no fighters. What a difference from the previous mission.

My next two missions were both to Frankfurt. On January 24th we took off before daylight and climbed through clouds to form the Group on top. It was quite a mess, hundreds of airplanes were milling around on top of the overcast looking for their Group. We finally got formed up and headed for Frankfurt. The mission was recalled before we got to the target because of weather, so we bombed a target of opportunity on the way back. Our specified target in Frankfurt was the Deutsche Metallwerke, the largest manufacturer of aircraft propellers in Germany.

We briefed again for the same target on the 26th of January, but the mission was scrubbed before take off time. We still went through all of the preparation and tension and the early rising. We flew a practice mission over England later that day and again on the 28th of January. Our Group Commander, Colonel Whittan, wanted to keep us proficient in formation flying.

We finally got off on another mission to Frankfurt on the 29th of January 1944. Our briefing was at 0400 and that meant that we had to get all ready and through with our breakfast and into the briefing room before 0400. (It is no wonder that I wake up so early now.) We were airborne by 0730. Weather again proved to be a problem over the target and we bombed through the clouds using a Pathfinder radar plane as the lead plane. The radar was primitive in those days. We encountered pretty heavy Flak. We carried 2300 gallons of fuel and ten 500 lb. bombs. We had to let down through the overcast when we came back home.

The very next day, 30th of January, we went to Brunswick. This one was my 7th mission. Briefing was not until 0530, so it was not quite as early a wake-up for us. We had a nice take off and forming of the Group. We were in VFR (visual flight rules) conditions, so we could see what we were doing during the time the Group was getting into formation. During VFR conditions, we took off at 5 second intervals and the lead airplane made a gradual turn after he was airborne and we just cut across the inside of the turn to catch him. Forming the group was easy when we could see each other.

We carried 2300 gallons of fuel and 42 incendiaries on that trip. After we got to altitude (24,000 ft.), we were all producing dense persistent condensation trails. That made formation flying a little more difficult since we could get into the con trails of the aircraft ahead of us. Our Navigator, John Hickey, accidentally disconnected his oxygen hose and he passed out before our bombardier, George Parkes, noticed it. We could have lost him if it had not been discovered in time. Dense cloud cover over the target, and most of Germany prevented the fighters from taking off, so we did not encounter fighters on this mission, but we had to bomb through the clouds again, using Pathfinder as our lead aircraft.

After all of that scrambling around, we got a 3-day pass to go to London. WOW, we could let off a little steam and relax for a couple of days. While we were lollygagging around in London, another crew flew our aircraft "Dolly" and they were shot down on another raid to Frankfurt on February 4th. I had flown in "Dolly" for my first seven missions.

On that Frankfurt mission that "Dolly" was shot down, one of the pilots (Maurice Crosbie, "Bing" to us) from our hut was hit in the left side of his face by Flak and parts of his face and his left eye were torn away. They were 23 minutes from the target when he was hit. The copilot flew the aircraft to the target area while the navigator dressed the wound. They both thought Bing was dying, but he stayed conscious and helped the copilot with the controls while they were on the bomb run. They finally got him out of the pilot's seat and laid him down on the floor on the deck below. I later saw the tough old birdman at a reunion of the 390th Veterans. He had a glass eye and the repairs to his face were hardly noticeable. We had quite a chat at the banquet.

I also met one of the airmen who was on "Dolly" when that aircraft was shot down. He was at a reunion of the 390th Memorial Foundation here in Tucson. Several of the local veterans had been asked to give a talk at one of the gatherings and I told the story of "Dolly" getting shot down. Mel Merrick came up to me afterward and said that he was on that aircraft when she was shot down. He bailed out and was taken prisoner and held in Stalag-Luft for about 19 months.

The next day, February 5, 1944, when we got back from our trip to London, we took off at dawn to bomb a German airfield at Villacoublay, France. The target was under cloud cover, so we bombed our secondary target, an airfield near Paris. I could see Notre Dame Cathedral as we flew toward the target. That was a thrill for me, a kid from a small town in Ohio. The airplane that we flew that day was named "Johnny Walker". It was the only B-17 that I flew on combat missions that made it back to the States in 1945.

The next day we were briefed on the same target and took off at dawn again. The target was obscured by clouds again. We flew all over France looking for a target of opportunity and ended up by bringing our bombs back home. That was not a very happy feeling, coming back home with the bombs still in the bomb bay. I didn't feel too comfy landing with twelve 500 lb. bombs under my fanny. The aircraft that we flew that day was "Yankee Doodle Dandy". It had been christened by James Cagney, a Hollywood star, and I was present when the aircraft was christened. That aircraft was shot down a few months after I flew it; four of the crew were killed and six were taken prisoner by the Germans.

The 10th of February we went back to Brunswick. We had tried twice before, but we really hit the target this time. German fighter planes were thick all the way in and out. My notes on that day were that "we saw seven B-17's go down and several fighters". The 8th Air Force lost 31 heavy bombers that day. The Combat Wing to our right was hit hard by the German fighters. It was a rough trip. That was my 10th mission. I was really a seasoned veteran by that time. I had over 68 hours of combat flying time plus numerous practice missions over England. I only had 15 more to go for that magic 25. That mission was in an aircraft named "Gloria Ann". I was awarded the 1st oak leaf cluster on my Air Medal after that mission.

We were then assigned the aircraft "Geronimo" as our aircraft. It had belonged to the crew that was shot down in good old "Dolly" while we were on pass. The reason that they took "Dolly" on the day they were shot down was because "Geronimo" was battle damaged and not flyable. When the ground crew got it all fixed again it became our aircraft. Our "Dolly" had been a B-17G and "Geronimo" was a B-17F, an earlier model. It flew OK, but there were some changes in the G model that made it easier to fly and the G also had the "chin turret" under the nose of the aircraft. The "chin turret" provided better defense from a frontal attack by enemy fighters. From then on, we flew Geronimo, if it was capable of flying, whenever we were chosen to fly a mission.

My oldest brother, Vernon, had been drafted and was serving in the Field Artillery. He had seen a lot of service by this time. He had been in the African campaign, the invasion of Sicily, the invasion of Italy and the Italian campaign. He had then been shipped to England to be in position for the invasion of Normandy.

I found out through V-mail from my parents that he was in England and finally located his unit. I went over to his location for a visit and then made plans for him to come over to our base. He came over and spent several days at our base in Framlingham. I had a bunk for him in the Quonset hut with the enlisted men from our crew. He was a Staff Sergeant and, even though he was my brother, he could not sleep in our hut. I did dress him in one of my jackets and take him to our club to eat. I even smuggled him into briefing one morning. He sat through the briefing and then rode out to the airplane with us and watched us prepare the airplane for the mission. When the armament man pulled the safety cotter pins from our bombs, he asked for one of them and labeled it with our destination. The target for that day was Brunswick. The pin is presently in a scrapbook that my son, Rick, has.

While Vernon was there, he flew on a practice mission with us around England and got to observe his baby brother flying that big old airplane in formation. I showed off just a little for him. We had a nice visit. We had not seen each other for a couple of years while he was off fighting and I was involved with pilot training.

Chapter 9
Combat over Germany

February 13th was our first mission in Geronimo. It was a nice neat mission; target was Crequy-Ruisseauville in France. We carried twelve 500 lb. bombs and stayed at an altitude of only 12,000 feet. We only carried 1,700 gallons of fuel, so we could carry extra bombs. Flak was meager and we did not see any enemy fighters, it was a real "milk-run". My comment in my diary was "I really enjoyed it."

That night the Germans raided Ipswich, which was only about 25 miles from our base. We sat on the top of our air raid shelter and watched the raid. We counted 14 aircraft shot down by English anti-aircraft fire. It was quite a show with searchlights and anti-aircraft fire and all of the aircraft falling out of the sky. For once we could see flak and not be on the receiving end of it.

The next day we slept late and flew a practice mission in the afternoon, a nice lazy day. We flew another practice mission on the 15th; we had to keep that formation flying nice and tight. A tight formation saved lives because of the combined firepower that we presented to the German fighter pilots.

February 16th we flew an air-sea rescue mission. It did not count as a combat mission. We were assigned a grid on the North Sea to search for English aircrews who had ditched the night before. We flew back and forth over our assigned grid looking for life rafts. During our flight, after about an hour out over the water, our bombardier, George Parkes, called me on the intercom and asked what my altimeter read. I told him, "It reads 50 feet above sea level, why do you ask?" He said, "Well, mine reads 50 feet below sea level and I was just wondering if we were in a submarine." We all got a good chuckle out of that interchange. We were flying pretty close to the top of the waves, but definitely not beneath them.

We flew a short practice mission on the 17th and then had a couple of days off. There were always duties for us on our days off. We had to censor mail and lots of other things that they thought up to keep us out of trouble. Our shower room was about ½ mile from our hut and it was not heated so, as your can imagine, we did not take a shower very often. The water was warm (sometimes) but the building was cold. I am afraid that our hygiene would not pass many standards. The nearest toilet and washbasin was about 100 feet from our hut. We could get water and heat it in a tin can on our pot-bellied stove in our hut if we had any fuel to burn in our stove. Living conditions were not the best, but they beat living in a foxhole.

On the 20th of February, we were awakened at 1:45 AM and started our preparations. Our target for the day was a German aircraft factory located at Posnan, Poland. We flew up over the North Sea and over Denmark and headed down into Poland, but we ran into weather and turned back. We bombed Rostock, Germany and our bombs did tremendous damage to the Neptumwerft shipyard and we also hit the Heinkel assembly plant. Our group was credited with 4 enemy aircraft shot down, 2 probable and 5 damaged. One of our aircraft ran low on fuel and flew into Sweden and the crew was interned there for the rest of the war. (Not bad duty.)

The next day, another early get up, briefing, preparation and take off and our crew had to abort part way over the North Sea. Our target was Brunswick and a pretty long haul and we sprung a leak in our oxygen system and had to turn back home. It was our first aborted mission, and none of us wanted to do that. After all of the work getting that far, we would rather go on and get it over with rather than go back home and not get credit for a mission. We logged 4 hours of combat time, but it did not count as a mission. That was to be my 13th (I called it 12B) but I still had that to face.

The 22nd and 23rd of February we did all of the preparation and the mission was scrubbed before takeoff each day. In a way, it was a relief not to go, but we had done all of the work and got no results. We would be out at the airplane with everything ready to start engines and then a red flare would zoom up into the air from the tower and the mission was scrubbed. We would then get everything out of the airplane and go back, turn in our chutes, oxygen masks and equipment and go back to the hut.

February 24th, we briefed on Posnan, Poland again. We got almost there, but the weather was terrible and we turned back and, guess what, we bombed Rostock again. Rostock was also under the cloud deck and the bomb release in the pathfinder aircraft malfunctioned. The group bombed through the clouds on a signal from the pathfinder aircraft and could not see the results, but a large column of black smoke rose through the clouds. Eight of the 25 enemy planes seen that day made vicious attacks and 3 were shot down. That was my longest mission, 11 hours and 20 minutes of flying time.

February 25th, target was an aircraft factory at Regensburg, deep in Germany. The factory had been seriously damaged six months previously and the Germans had been busy rebuilding it during those six months. The weather was great and we hit our target on the nose, resulting in the target being eliminated from priority status. Our total flying time that day was 9:30, another long mission. We had been alerted for seven straight days and had flown on four of them. That was the time that the commander said, in the morning briefing, "We are wearing the Luft Waffe down." I said to myself, "Sure we are. We have been awakened in the middle of the night seven days in a row, flown like crazy, and all of the work getting ready to fly and *we are wearing them down?*" I suspected that it was we who were wearing down. I know that I was worn out after that week.

Chapter 10
Combat over Germany

We went to London on a three-day pass. We blew off some steam and relaxed for a few days -- It was great. We saw some shows and visited some pubs and chased a few girls. The war was still going on and we could tell. London was blacked out completely every night and there were air raid alerts almost every night. There were enemy planes a couple of nights and we sometimes had the buzz bombs hit when we were there.

Our next mission (March 2nd) was on an airfield used for advanced pilot training by the Germans. It was located near Chartres, France. The bombardiers were cautioned that there was a revered shrine close to the target and that they should be sure of their target. When we got there, the target area was obscured by clouds, so we attempted to bomb the secondary target at Cormeilles-en-Vixin, but here also clouds obscured the target. The 390th lost one aircraft at Abbeville where the flak was extremely accurate. Some of us brought our bombs back. We landed at Framlingham after dark. Our briefing had been at noon. That was my 15th mission and I was awarded the 2nd cluster on the Air Medal.

The next day, March 3, 1944, we were routed out of bed early. We did our normal routine, clean up, shave and go to breakfast. We would always be able to tell if we were to be going on an especially rough mission, because we would get fresh eggs for breakfast. The normal eggs were powdered and not very good. This morning we got fresh eggs, so we knew that the mission was to be a rough one. When we got to briefing and the curtains were pulled back from the target board, we saw that our target for the day was BERLIN. You could hear the gasps from the crew members when we saw that we were really going to try for the *BIG CITY,* the capital of the German Empire. Our target was an electrical equipment manufacturing company on the edge of Berlin.

The weather was terrible, we ran into dense cloud cover and it went all the way up to our altitude. The entire Eight Air Force was recalled. We turned around and came back home. We were into Denmark when we turned around and came back. We encountered flak, but no fighters. The 95th Bomb Group and part of the 100th Bomb Group ignored the recall and continued on to Berlin. They were the first US AAF bombers over Berlin. I think that they were just hot-rodding it. They claimed that they thought the recall was done by the Germans. We, the guys who obeyed orders, came back to England and brought our bombs back. Again, we had to land with a bomb bay full of bombs, not a sporty proposition.

The 4th of March we briefed on the same target and tried again for Berlin. The results were about the same for the 390th, but not for our crew. We lost our #2 engine when we were about 40 miles into France and returned to Framlingham. The Group went a little further and then turned back, bringing their bombs back with them. I made a note in my diary that it was foolish to send a force out on that mission, since the weather was about the same as the day before. The total flight time for our crew that day was 5 hours and 5 minutes. The entire group was in the air a little longer. A lot of the time was spent getting into formation and into our correct spot in the force. We took off in a snowstorm that morning. All that work and we had to abort.

The next day, March 5, was a day off except for a practice mission. We only flew 2 hours. Sleeping in and getting up at a reasonable time made it seem like a day of leisure, but we were just preparing for the next day.

The 3rd and 4th of March we flew the aircraft named Geronimo. A few days later, it was still out of commission so we flew "Wild Children" on the raid on the 6th of March. That was the first full daylight raid on Berlin. Our target was the same as the two previous attempts, the Bosch electrical equipment manufacturing company. The Germans were well aware of where we were going and had certainly prepared for us. They put up everything that they could that day to prevent us from bombing in and around the city of Berlin. The Eighth Air Force succeeded in getting to the target, but at a terrible cost. There were 69 heavy bombers lost from the force that the Eighth put up that day. The German fighters were everywhere. It was estimated that the Eighth Air Force was attacked by 600 enemy fighters that day, on our way into the target and out. My notes in my diary for that day were "We were really out to get the big town this time. Weather fine. I saw more flak and fighters than I ever saw before. We were under fighter attack for 5 hours. Really a rough day. Large losses."

When we were on our bomb run, the lead bombardier could not see the target because of the haze and smoke from the previous bomb groups, so he elected to fly over the Bosch factory and try for another factory in the Spandau district of Berlin. Most of our bombs fell into a built-up area along the Navel River. The Flak over the Berlin area was intense. The old expression, "so thick that you could get out of your airplane and walk on it" came to mind as we approached Berlin and then as we flew over the city. Records that we now have indicate that the Germans had 6,220 heavy anti-aircraft cannons at that time, and I think that they all shot at us.

Our group only lost one plane over Germany. One other, "Gloria Ann", made it back to Framlingham and crashed on the base. The airplane was salvaged. It had over 700 holes in it from 20MM cannon fire from fighter aircraft. The great news was that everyone walked away from that airplane after the crash. I had flown "Gloria Ann" on my 10th mission and this mission was my 18th.

Our group was credited with 27 enemy fighters destroyed, 2 probably destroyed and 3 damaged on that mission. The flying time our crew logged on that mission was 8:00 hours.

The 100th Bomb Group, which was in the same Wing as our Bomb Group, lost 15 out of a total of 30 aircraft that day --- terrible losses. The loss for the Eighth Air force, 69 heavy bombers, was the worst ever for any single day. In addition to the enemy fighters, the Flak was extremely heavy over Berlin. That was the only time that the German fighters left us alone, when we were in the heavy Flak. I attributed our lack of losses to the tight formation that the 390th flew. We presented a lot of firepower from our 50 caliber machine guns when we flew in our proper positions and stayed close. I think the German fighter pilots would look at our tight formation and go hit another group. The aircraft that we flew that day was "Wild Children".

On the 7th of March we were routed out of bed at 0530 and went through the gyrations of getting ready to fly. We had just gotten into the briefing room and the mission was scrubbed because of weather. It was sort of like a day off for us and we really needed it.

The 390th went back to Berlin on the 8th of March, but our crew was not tasked to fly on that mission. The Group lost three aircraft on the way to the target on that day.

Our next mission was on the 9th of March and it was back to the "BIG TOWN". Our target for the day was the Heinkel aircraft components factory. We had complete cloud cover on our route into the target and over the target, so we bombed through the clouds using a pathfinder radar aircraft. We could not identify our primary target with the dense cloud cover, so the pathfinder chose to bomb the Friedrichstrasse railway station in Berlin. We could not see the results of our bombing, but when we were near Brunswick on our way home, a large black column of smoke could be seen rising from Berlin 100 miles away. We must have hit something that burned fiercely.

Because of the cloud cover over most of Germany, we encountered no fighters. It was certainly different from the 6th of March. The Flak over the target was intense as it was before. I later found out that the Germans had 88MM, 105MM and 128MM anti-aircraft guns in the Berlin area. Any of them could reach us, but the bigger ones put out a lot more shrapnel. We jokingly called this mission another milk run because of the lack of fighters. Our flight time for this mission was 8 hours and 45 minutes. The airplane that we flew on this mission was "Wild Children". Four months later, "Wild Children" crashed and all 10 crewmembers were killed.

Chapter 11
Combat over Germany

About the time that I finished my 18th mission the good news was passed out that they were extending the tour of combat from 25 missions to 30 missions. You can imagine what that did to morale. We all had a goal in mind, if we could survive through 25 missions we could go home (back to God's country). Now the completion target had to be moved out and survival had to be hoped for for a longer time. Since I already had 18 missions, they pro-rated my tour to 28 instead of 30. That was some relief, but still a blow to the morale. Several of the crew had more missions than I had because they had some under their belts when I joined them, so some of them were still on the 25-mission list.

Our navigator, Hickey, had been selected for Squadron Navigator and had moved out of our hut and off of our crew. George Parkes, our bombardier, had been told that he was our new navigator. He said, "I don't know anything about navigating." but he was told that that was his job and he should keep a log of everything that happened and record where we were if he could tell. He did that and his first few logs were pretty skimpy, but he eventually got with the program and started keeping better logs.

The log was a record of a lot of things that happened to us after we took off. He recorded our form-up with the rest of the group and our climb to altitude. Our crossing of the enemy coast was recorded and then flak and fighter activity was a part of the log. Every aircraft that we saw go down was recorded and how many chutes we saw from each aircraft. Information like that helped determine how many members of the crew potentially ended up as POW's. We were all debriefed by intelligence officers when we got back to the base and all of the collective information was put together to compile a pretty good picture of what happened on the mission.

The debriefing took place in a room where there were 4 or 5 tables with 11 seats around them, 1 for the intelligence officer and 10 for the crew. All of the crews could not be debriefed at once, so we waited around until our turn. I remember the Red Cross ladies there with coffee and donuts, which were welcome. After a really rough mission, the Flight Surgeon would be waiting at the door to the debriefing room and he would have a table full of GI tin-cups and some bottles of Scotch whiskey. He would pour a small ration of that good booze into the cups and hand one to each crew member as we waited to get into the debriefing. (I was only 20 years old and some of our gunners were still in their teens, but the Flight Surgeon, in his infinite wisdom, thought that a good shot of Scotch would be good for us after our harrowing experiences of the day.) On a couple of the previous rough missions, I noted that two of the crew, for some reason, did not take their drink of Scotch. I remembered that, and after one particular rough mission, and I asked them to take their shot and pour it into my cup. They did, and as we were standing there waiting to get to a debriefing table, I slugged away at the raw Scotch whiskey. We had been up for a long time and breakfast had been many hours ago and the Scotch really hit me hard. By the time we got to the table for debriefing, my speech was slightly slurred and by the time we finished the debriefing, I could hardly walk. That was the last time that I asked for extra rations on the booze.

After my 19th mission (Berlin) we had a few days off. We went to London every chance we had. We went to some nice places in London and crawled a few pubs. I met a nice girl who was an usher in a movie theater. We dated a few times when I could get into London. I took her some nice presents like soap, candy bars and a large piece of nylon from a parachute. Those things were difficult to get in wartime England. She appreciated them. We never did get too serious.

After our pass to London we started flying practice missions every day. The weather over the continent must have been bad so we really concentrated on our formation flying.

According to my flight log I flew 9 practice missions from the 10th through the 22nd of March. I also had my 21st birthday on the 21st of March 1944. I was now an experienced combat veteran with 19 missions under my belt and was old enough to vote and buy a drink. I felt a lot older than 21. I had crammed a lot of interesting and exciting experiences into the last two years.

On March 23, I flew my 20th mission. The target was Brunswick (Braunschweig to the Germans). The weather was still bad over the continent and we were over cloud cover all the way. We bombed on a pathfinder aircraft using his radar. We saw lots of fighters, but our group was not attacked. Our practice formation flying may have paid off. Flak was intense over the target area and on the way back, but we did not lose any aircraft from our group. We put up 30 aircraft for that mission. My comment in my little diary was that we came through "Happy Valley" on the way home. I would assume that I was referring to the Ruhr Valley, which was a heavy industrial area for the Germans and had tremendous anti-aircraft installations. Our #3 prop governor was acting up all the way, but we were able to stay with the formation and complete our mission.

My only comment in my diary for the 25th of March was "Bud took his long johns off." Bud was referring to Norman Palmer, the pilot of our crew. It must have been an exceptionally warm day in England for Bud to take such drastic action or maybe the long johns needed laundering. Our facilities were far from adequate for doing laundry. I have chuckled about that diary entry many times since I found my diary 60 years after I wrote in it.

My 21st mission was on the 26th of March and the target was La Glacerie, a German rocket site. We got up early and briefed for a mission on Leipzig, but that mission was scrubbed. My notes do not tell why it was scrubbed, but I would assume that the weather was bad over Germany. The weather was perfect over the secondary target and our squadron hit the target. My notes are "Nice milk run. Not much flak. No fighters." George Parkes, our bombardier (changed to navigator) finished his missions on this raid. George and I had become quite good buddies and went to town together when we were off duty.

The next day, March 27th, we bombed a German airfield at Cazaux. It was a beautifully planned mission. We bombed from a lower altitude, 12,000. The weather was perfect. We had fighter support all the way. We saw no German fighters and the flak was moderate.

The airfield was an important base for the operation of the HE-177 German bombers. Our group put up 34 ships that day, divided into two groups, A and B. The A group hit the target with 500 pound bombs and the B group dropped incendiaries. I used to say that the first bombs made the kindling and then the incendiaries set it on fire. The hangers, workshops and fuel storage facilities were severely damaged.

March 28th, my 23rd mission was "Another nice raid." The target was another German airfield located near Chateaudun. The altitude for our flight was 18,000. We had good fighter support all the way and saw no enemy fighters. The flak over the target was "very accurate". Bud Palmer finished his 25th mission on this trip, but he had one more to fly because of the extension.

Herbie, our top turret gunner and flight engineer, took a hit on one of the missions about in this time period. He was in the top turret and screamed, "I got hit in the ass ---- I got hit in the ass." I was busy and could not get to him to see if he needed first aid so I called for the navigator to come up and check him out. George Parkes came up and checked him and when he went back down and plugged into his intercom and oxygen again he was laughing. He reported that Herbie was not bleeding, but that the piece of flak had hit him in the right rear hard enough to go through five layers of clothing and drop into Herbie's right rear hip pocket. It was a large jagged piece of flak and must have been falling through the air when we ran into it and it came through metal parts of the airplane and hit Herbie.

When we landed and taxied onto our hard stand there was a reporter from the Stars and Stripes (the overseas newspaper) running from airplane to airplane asking if there was a story. I called down to him to wait for us to get out of the airplane and that we had a good one for him. He waited and all ten of us gathered at the front of the aircraft and told him the story of Herbie getting hit in the ass. We were all laughing about it. It got into the paper, but it was slightly revised. It said that Herbie caught his souvenir of the war in his hip pocket. Herbie did not bleed, so he did not get a Purple Heart. He did have a big bruise on his butt where the chunk of flak hit him.

My notes in my diary for the 28th of March say, "White flag is up tonight." When the white flag was flying in the squadron area it meant that our squadron was not scheduled to fly the next day. We could use a few days off.

The next day, March 29th, my comment in my dairy was, "Bud put his long johns back on." It never did stay warm for very long at that time of the year in England.

March 30th was a relaxing day off. We were alerted in the evening that we would be flying the next day. The red flag was flying in the squadron area. I had talked with Major Pennebaker, our squadron operations officer about getting checked out as first pilot and finishing my tour as aircraft commander. He had given his approval for a check-out flight. I was an old 21 by then.

April 1st we briefed on Ludwigshaven again. The target there was a production plant for synthetic oil. We got all formed and got into the continent as far as the eastern edge of Belgium and encountered a solid weather front. The heavy clouds were up to 18,000 feet with another layer starting at about 20,000. As we proceeded, it became apparent that we were not going to be able to keep our formation together in the clouds. The message was sent back to England and the 26 aircraft were recalled to base, so we turned around and went home to Framlingham. That was Bud's 26th mission and his last one. He was finished and eligible to return to God's Country.

"Geronimo"
Cocky 21 year old
Just checked out as
1st Pilot

Chapter 12
Check-out as 1st Pilot - Finish 28 Missions

Major Pennebaker kept his promise about checking me out as first pilot. He took me out to the airfield, we got into a B-17 that he selected, and he had me fly the left seat and do everything that the aircraft commander would be required to do. We found another B-17 flying around over England and he told me to hook onto his wing and fly formation with him. I did and flew nice tight formation until he said to break it off and head home. I found Framlingham, landed the aircraft smoothly, put it back into the hard stand, and shut everything down. Major Pennebaker said, "OK. You are checked out. You will keep the same crew number as Palmer had."

Some of the old crew had not finished, so they were assigned to my crew and the rest of the crew positions were filled by people who had not finished their missions for one reason or another. We were not the close-knit crew that I had been used to flying with, but we got along fine. I had four missions to go and I wanted to do it in style.

My first mission as first pilot was Reime, but we could not get to the target because of weather, so we bombed an airfield at Maldegem, Belgium. It was the 10th of April 1944. We scored hits on the hangers, work shops and dispersal area. We saw no enemy fighters and the flak was moderate. This was my 25th mission. I had 3 more to go and they were to be done in the next three days. I didn't know that at that time.

April 11th we had an early briefing on an old favorite, the German aircraft factory at Posnan, Poland. It was a long distance to Posnan, so we started early. Again we ran into severe weather after we got into Poland and could not get to the target. Again we bombed our secondary target, Rostock. We tried to hit the

Heinkel aircraft assembly works, but due to cloud conditions, most of our bombs hit to the southeast of the target, into the town. We encountered JU-88 German fighters, which fired rockets at us. They were not very successful. We had heavy flak over the Rostock area.

That was my third attempt at Posnan and each time we bombed Rostock. I kid about it today at the 390th Memorial Museum, where I am a docent. I say that I would guess that the people in Rostock were saying, "I sure wish that the weather in Poland would clear up so those Yanks would quit bombing us and go bomb Posnan."

The aircraft factory at Posnan remained, until the end of the war, one of the few critical factories that the Eighth Air Force was not able to bomb. When the Russians captured it, they found rows of parked aircraft.

My 20th through the 26th missions were flown in good old Geronimo. Three months after my last mission in Geronimo, it was shot down and all ten crew members were killed.

April 12th we briefed on Leipzig. Weather was stinko over England and as we tried to form the group we had to descend to keep out of the clouds. The group then climbed as we proceeded over the North Sea. As we got into Belgium we ran into more dense clouds, which made formation flying very dangerous, nearly impossible. The mission was recalled and we all returned to England. We were not sure that they were going to count that as a mission. It was several days later that the decision was made that it would count. The rationale was that, although we brought our bombs back, anti-aircraft guns did shoot at us. Boy, was I glad that they decided to count that one, because that made my next one my last one. I did not know that my last one was my last one until several days after I had flown it. That was because they delayed making the decision to count the April 12th mission. I was really "sweating it out".

My last mission is a story all unto itself. The mission was a long one, to Augsburg, deep in southeast Germany. It was April 13th, maybe I called it April 12B. I was a little superstitious. The aircraft factory there had been hit before, but was back into full production by the 13th of April.

We did not encounter any enemy fighters on that trip, but the flak was intense. Our group lost 3 aircraft over the target. One of them was badly damaged, but still flying and it went to Switzerland. We could see the lake on the border of Switzerland from the target area. The crew of that aircraft was interned by the Swiss and had to spend the rest of the war in Switzerland living in a hotel. *Tough duty.*

I was flying "Belle of the Brawl" since "Geronimo" was still out of commission. We took a few hits over the target, one of them being somewhere in our #1 engine. It started leaking oil. The ball turret gunner called the leak to me. We kept a close watch on the oil pressure as we progressed away from Augsburg, headed home. The leak appeared to be rather minor, but we had to watch closely because the engine oil was also used to control our propeller. We got all the way to Belgium and #1 was still running. As we approached Brussels there was a huge storm towering over the area. Two groups went to the south of the storm and one group (us) went to the north of the storm. Our path took us directly over the airfield at Brussels. The airfield was heavily defended by flak and those gunners were highly skilled. The first burst and all succeeding bursts were right in the formation. Of the 38 planes that went over the airport, 13 suffered extensive damage, 9 had moderate damage and 13 had slight damage. Almost every plane was hit.

Our plane was hit in #2 and #3 engine oil coolers. The oil cooler was like a radiator that cooled our engine oil, so a hit there was very serious. The ball turret gunner called in the leaks and in a minute or two his turret was covered with oil and he could no longer see out, so I got him out of there. I had the flight engineer stand between the pilots' seats and keep his eye on the oil pressures. I told him that if he saw either of those two engine oil pressures start to drop he was to punch the feather button for that engine immediately. Engine oil controlled the prop and if he caught it soon enough we would have enough oil left to feather the prop. (Feathering the prop meant to turn the blades so that the leading edge of the prop was facing forward. We could then shut down the engine, the prop would stand still and we would have reduced the drag.)

Number 2 oil pressure started to drop and he hit the feather button. The prop feathered and I shut down #2. Moments later, #3 oil pressure started to drop and he hit #3 feather button -- - TOO LATE. We had lost too much oil and the feather pump did not have enough oil to feather the prop. Our #3 engine was no longer producing power; it was wind milling. Our forward motion was causing the prop to turn. It caused a lot of resistance. In just a few minutes the engine "froze". It locked up because of lack of oil to the pistons. The force of the spinning prop tore the gears loose in the nose of the engine and the prop was then spinning wildly, again being driven by our forward motion and creating a lot of drag.

I had to leave the formation and I headed straight for Framlingham. Fortunately we were not too far from the coastline when we were hit. We also had some altitude and I began a gradual descent. Everything was going OK and it looked like we would get to Framlingham with a little luck. We were still leaking oil from #1 engine, but the leak was moderate and the engine was still running.

Our procedure was to shoot a red flare through the flare port in the top of the aircraft for wounded on board and a green flare for mechanical difficulty. When I got to the base, it looked like Christmas over the base. Red, green and red/green combination flares were being fired from lots of aircraft. The hits had been bad over Brussels.

I ended up being #5 to land and I kept a little extra airspeed on the final approach because of having only 2 engines running, so I landed a little hotter than normal. We only had slightly over 6300 feet of runway, so with the extra speed I landed OK, but I was really moving. I touched my brakes and found out that I had no brakes. They were shot out, too. I was moving quite a bit faster than normal and wishing that I had an anchor to throw out. As I approached the end of the runway, it was obvious that I was going off if I didn't do something and quickly. I put full power on the #1 engine and turned the aircraft to the right. As I got turned 90 degrees to my right I put full power on the #4 engine to straighten the aircraft and then full power on both of them to get me clear of the runway. The good old English mud stopped my aircraft. The main landing gear was buried in the mud about a foot and a half. All 10 of us really felt like kissing that good old mud, we were so glad to get down safely. I found out later that that was my last mission and *was I ever glad.*

Belle of the Brawl was so badly damaged that it was out of commission for quite a few days for repair. Three weeks after I flew it to Augsburg, it was shot down. Two of the crew got out and were taken prisoner, the rest of the crew were killed. I had missed another, LUCKY ME!!

I was awarded the Distinguished Flying Cross after that last mission. I was also promoted to 1st Lieutenant. The important thing was that I was now eligible to return to the States.

While I waited around for orders to proceed home, I flew three more flights in B-17's. Two of them were with new crews and I flew as instructor pilot with them to check them out on the proper method of flying formation and our local procedures. One flight was a test flight on a B-17 that had a new engine installed. When a new engine was installed, we flew the aircraft to check out the new engine and got a couple of hours on it to insure it was operating OK before it was sent into combat. The one that I flew had a run-away turbo on take off, just about the time that I broke free of the ground. The manifold pressure went sky high and the top three cylinders blew right off of the engine. One of them came part way through the cowl. That made for an interesting flight; I had to shut down the new engine and feather the prop right after take-off. The total flight only lasted 20 minutes, but it was an interesting 20 minutes. The aircraft needed another new engine.

A summary of the B-17s that I flew on Combat Missions:

Dolly   Shot down Feb 44 – 10 POW
Yankee Doodle Dandy Shot down May 44--4KIA-6POW
Gloria Ann   Crashed March 44 ---10 Survived
Geronimo   Shot down July 44---10 KIA
Wild Children   Crashed July 44----10 KLD
Belle of the Brawl Shot down May 44 --8 KIA-2 POW
Johnny Walker   Survived

Chapter 13 (12B)
Back to the States

I finally got orders to proceed to another base in England for shipment home. I arrived there late in the evening and was assigned to a room in the Officers' Quarters. I went to my room and there were two bunks, upper and lower. Someone had already occupied the top bunk, so I threw my stuff on the bottom bunk and went over to the Officer's Club. After dinner and a couple of drinks, I went back to my room. The guy in the top bunk was there. I introduced myself and found out that my roommate was Captain Don Gentile, who was the leading Ace in the U.S. Army Air Forces in Europe. He had 20 kills. He and his wingman, Captain John Godfrey, were being sent back to the States for a war bond drive. I was pleased to have Gentile as my "top cover" for the few days that we were there. He was later killed on a test flight at Wright Field and a base nearby was named after him. His home was in Piqua, Ohio, not far from my hometown.

After enough people were gathered to fill a troop ship we departed Merry England for the States. We were on a much smaller ship than the one on which we had gone over to England. We came home in convoy with lots of other ships. There were Naval vessels patrolling all around the convoy checking for subs. Several times, during the 14 days it took us to get to the States, the destroyers dropped depth charges. We knew there were sub packs out there and we guessed that subs had been spotted on the sonar equipment. The Navy guys may have just been trying to give us a thrill; who knows? Anyhow, after 14 days at sea we came into New York harbor. We were really impressed as we passed the Statue of Liberty. As we came into the dock area there were all kinds of boats tooting their horns and there was a band playing on the dock and lots of people to greet the ship as she docked. We really felt like a bunch of heroes. It was a real thrill for all of us as the tugboats maneuvered us into the dock.

Several of us, who had become friendly on the ship during our 14 day trip, stayed together in New York and had a ball for a few days before proceeding home. We went to Coney Island one day and rode all the rides. We were treated like real heroes all during our stay in the Big Apple. We could not pay for a drink anywhere. There was always someone picking up the tab. We stayed in a really nice hotel in New York and my room bill was $3.50 per day. A far cry from hotel prices in New York today.

Harry James and his orchestra were performing on the top floor of our hotel, so we spent one enjoyable evening up there listening to the band. Don Gentile and his wing-man were up there that night. The wing-man, Godfrey, was a very flamboyant individual, quite different from Gentile. He ended up on the stage with the band and actually had a trumpet in his hand. I don't think it was Harry James's trumpet, but it could have been. The crowd got quite a kick out of him. I kept reading about the two of them, later, when they were on the war bond drive all over the country.

The trip home from New York was by train and I ended up on an army base in Indiana, not far from my home in St. Marys, Ohio. I don't remember how I got on an army base, but I called home and asked my dad if he could come over and get me. Mom and Dad drove over and picked me up and we drove back to St. Marys. There was a lot of rejoicing and hugging in that meeting. I was glad to be back into familiar territory.

I had a couple of weeks leave at home. It gave me a chance to strut around town and show off. I had been awarded the Distinguished Flying Cross and four Air Medals. I was a decorated war hero and I felt like I was entitled to a little strutting. I was now old enough to buy a drink legally but it proved hard to do that in my hometown. There was always someone there to say, "This one's on me". It was an enjoyable couple of weeks.

During the time I was on leave, I went down to Wright

Field and visited the office where I had worked before I went into the Army Air Force. I was welcomed with open arms, literally; there was a lot of hugging. My old boss said, "Come on, let's go around to the Staff Offices where you used to deliver and pick up the classified correspondence. Most of the same people are still here." We went into the still familiar offices where I had gone many times and, sure enough, the same secretaries were there and again I was welcomed warmly. The Captain who had talked me into taking the Aviation Cadet exams was still there but he was now a Lieutenant Colonel. Most of the Chiefs of Staff were still there in the same positions as when I had worked there. There was one big difference though. They had all been Colonels when I was working there and now they were Major Generals. What a change, I had been a lowly civilian and they had been Colonels, now they were 2 star Generals and I was a 1st Lieutenant. I was still the lowly one, but it was different.

One of the secretaries, who had been my favorite, took me in to see "the boss". The Major General said, "Sure, I remember when he used to bring the classified in here. Sit down son and tell me about it. You have done more in this war than I have. I have been stuck behind this damn desk." I sat down (hardly relaxed, scared to death to be talking to a 2 star General.) He said, "What are you going to do now, and what do you want to do now?" I said that I was going down to Miami Beach for a week of R & R (rest and recuperation) and that I would probably be assigned as an instructor pilot somewhere and I didn't especially want to do that. I would like to be assigned to Wright Field. He scratched a little note on a pad on his desk and said, "You go on down to Miami and enjoy your week. When you get there, there will be orders for you to be assigned back here."

Wow, how good could it get? I was going to be assigned to Wright Field, only 60 miles from home. My time there as a GS nobody had paid off. At this time, it had been a little over two years since I had been sworn into the Army.

Our R&R at Miami Beach was great. We were put up in one of the luxury hotels right on the beach. There was a swimming pool with fresh water and the beach right behind the hotel with the beautiful ocean right there. They had all kinds of activities planned for us. We went deep-sea fishing and lazed around a lot. We were so pale from our months in England that we had to be really careful of the sun. The days were nice and warm and the evenings were balmy. My roommate and I rented a convertible and drove around with the top down the whole week. Boy, was that ever great for picking up the girls. We had a great time for the week that we were there. Sure enough, there were orders for me to be shipped to Wright Field.

Chapter 14
Back to Wright Field, Ohio

When I got back to Wright Field and checked in, they really didn't know what to do with me. All I knew how to do was fly a B-17 and drop bombs on the Germans. There wasn't much of that going on at Wright Field.

They finally decided to assign me to the Flight Test Section. A test flight was required on every aircraft that had major maintenance performed on it such as, engine change, structural repair or control surface replacement or repair. There were several aircraft assigned to Base Flight section and we could fly those when we were not doing a test flight, so I got checked out in several different aircraft and was having a good time flying around there. I wanted to be flying all the time, even when there was not a requirement for a test flight to be flown. One of the planes assigned there was a B-17 and no one was current as first pilot. I was still current from my time over in England, so I flew it quite a few flights as instructor pilot to get some of the local pilots current in the aircraft again.

There was a regulation in effect at that time that allowed a pilot to take the female members of his family on a flight in a military aircraft. I requested permission to take my mother up in the B-17. There was a lot of paper work involved to get permission, but I got it all done and Mom came down to Wright Field to go for a ride in a B-17. We took off with Mom standing behind the pilots' seats. There was no seat there and, of course, no seat belt. My co-pilot was a Major who wanted to get some time in the B-17 so Mom thought her son was really coming up in the world, having a Major for a copilot.

After take-off, I flew straight up to St. Marys, Ohio, our hometown. I flew all around there at fairly low altitude so Mom could see it all from the air. The Major was kind enough to get out of the co-pilot's seat and let Mom sit there. She was like a little kid in a candy store. It was the thrill of her life. We flew around the paper mill where Dad worked and lots of the employees came out to watch us. After cruising around the area near St. Marys for quite a while, I climbed up to about 8 or 9 thousand feet, which put us above the pretty cumulus clouds and flew around over the clouds for a few minutes then descended and started back to Wright Field. Mom had to give up her seat as co-pilot and the Major got back into the seat. On the landing, I bounced the airplane, not a good landing at all, by my standards, but Mom thought it was a great landing. It was a fun flight for me, showing off in front of my Mom.

One of the other airplanes that I checked out in there was the A-24. It was the Air Force designation for the Navy "Dauntless", a single engine dive-bomber. It was a fun airplane to fly, had quite a bit of power and was very maneuverable. I had not flown a single engine aircraft since Basic Flight School and I had a lot of fun doing all kinds of aerobatics in that plane. I took it up to St. Marys one nice sunny day and flew down low over the paper mill. I kept buzzing the place until I was sure that Dad was outside watching and then I gained a little altitude and started really showing off. I was doing slow rolls, snap rolls and loops. The first time I rolled over, one of the guys next to my Dad grabbed his arm and said, "Oh my God, Ben, he's gone upside down." Dad got a kick out of it and I enjoyed showing off in front of some of the hometown guys.

I was living in the BOQ (bachelor officer's quarters) and eating my meals in the snack bars or the Officer's Club. It was great living compared to what we had in England. One evening I joined another 1st lieutenant at a table and as we ate we got to talking and he said that he really needed to get down to Nashville, Tennessee. He was going to try to get train transportation the next day. I said, "I'll take you down as soon as we finish eating". That was great with him, so he got his bag and met me down at Base Operations. I got a map and filed a flight plan for Nashville, using one of the A-24 aircraft. The plane had two seats and there was plenty of room for his luggage. Off we went. It was a nice flight and we got there without incident. By the time we got there it was nearly dark and I had not flown any at night since B-17 training in Washington, so I did not feel comfortable about flying back to Wright Field at night. I went into Base Operations and sent a message back to Wright Field, "RON (Remain over night) Nashville, darkness" and sent my name and aircraft number.

I got up fairly early the next morning, had breakfast and filed a flight plan back to Wright Field. I flew back and arrived shortly after normal duty hours started. I parked the airplane and strolled into the flight test office. WOW! The Major who was in charge of the section was waiting for me. He ripped me up one side and down the other. He said, "What do you mean, just going out there and grabbing an aircraft and taking off without getting permission and orders to do that sort of a thing. That is not your private Air Force out there. You are not allowed to do that.' He raved and ranted for quite a while and I just stood there. When he finally calmed down I told him that over in England we didn't have to go through all those kinds of procedures to just fly an airplane. That started him up again and I was getting chewed out for another half hour. He finally wound down and gave up. I had learned that I just couldn't walk out to any airplane and take it wherever I wanted to go. It was a good lesson that things were done a little differently here in the States than they were overseas.

After a couple of weeks, I got a call from a Colonel in Personnel. He told me to come up and see him. His office was in the Headquarters area where I had worked as a civilian. I got up there quickly, went into his office, saluted, and stood there at attention. He said, "Sit down, son." (Here was this "son" stuff again.) He said, "I thought you might be interested in an opening that I have. There is one spot available in the class just getting ready to start at Air Force Service Command Central Test Pilot School. The school is located at Kelly Army Air Force Base at San Antonio, Texas. Would you be interested in attending that school?" I immediately envisioned myself zooming around in some exotic experimental types of aircraft, so I promptly said "YES SIR". He told me that I would have orders that day assigning me to the school as a student. I got my orders and cleared the base. I had a couple of days before I had to depart, so I went up to St. Marys to see my parents. I had found out that there was a cargo plane departing from Wright Field on a regular basis to Kelly Field, so I got a seat on that and it made my trip to Kelly very easy.

I checked in and was assigned a room in the BOQ. The room that I was assigned was in the building that was called "The Palace" It was one of the older, permanent buildings and was really nice. The Officers' Mess (dining room) was on the ground floor, so going to eat was really easy. I later found out that I was the only one of my class at the Test Pilots' School who had a room in the "Palace". The rest of them were assigned BOQ rooms in barracks style buildings. I figured that the Gods of War were really watching out for me. I also checked in at the school and found that the class was due to begin the next day.

Chapter 15
Test Pilot School

The school was designed to check us out as 1st pilot in a lot of different aircraft and to teach us the details of the systems on all of the aircraft. We had ground school ½ of each day and flying the other half. The aircraft that we were to check-out in were: A-20, A-24, A-25, B-17, B-24, B-25, B-26, P-39, P-40, P-63, T-6 and UC-78. All of these types of aircraft except the T-6 and the UC-78 were being used in combat at the time we went through the school.

There were quite a variety of aircraft and types so that we could handle many different situations that we would face as test pilots. The ground school was intensive and covered lots of systems that were common to several types of aircraft and then specific systems that may be unusual.

The method of check-out as 1st pilot in each aircraft was:

1. Study the systems for the aircraft involved.

2. Take a written test on the aircraft systems and handling characteristics.

3. Fly the aircraft (with an instructor pilot if possible).

Several of the aircraft we were to fly were single seat only with no room for an instructor. So our method of check-out was the same except the instructor pilot would stand on the wing and give us a test on our knowledge of the aircraft and its systems and then tell us to go fly it. Our first flight in these aircraft was a solo flight. The flying part of the school was fun, but the class room work and studying of the technical orders for each aircraft was hard work.

In the aircraft which had pilot/copilot positions, we would fly with another student after our original check-out with one of the instructors. The commandant of the school and I were the only two who had combat experience and there was a little jealousy among the students and the instructors. We didn't go around bragging about our experiences, but our decorations were a part of our uniform and I wore my ribbons. I had the DFC and Air Medal with 3 oak leaf clusters. After I had been there for a few days the commandant took me aside and suggested that it might be better for me to leave my ribbons off while I was in the school. It was all right for him to wear his because he was the commandant.

What a lot of fun we had flying those aircraft. The students would get together miles away from the field and have dog fights in the fighter types of our planes and fly formation with each other. There was also a lot of buzzing (going down low over someone or something). One of the students buzzed a boat out on a lake nearby and on his pull-up he hit an electrical cable that went across the lake. He took a chunk of the wing tip off, but made it back to base OK. Two of the students were flying formation and one of them rammed a pitot tube (a tube protruding from the wing tip that provided air-speed info to the cockpit gage) into the other guy's wing. Needless to say, the students were reprimanded soundly. The commandant had the authority to remove any of the students from the school.

My flight experience, which nearly got me washed out of the school or killed, was in the P-63, the airplane called the King Cobra. The King Cobra was a larger version of the P-39 Air Cobra and it had quite a bit more power. Both of them had the engine behind the pilot and the drive shaft to the prop ran between the pilot's legs. Each of them was equipped with a cannon that fired though the prop hub. Of course we were not doing any shooting in Texas, we were just trying to get the feel of the airplanes and try them in all sorts of maneuvers.

Each of our flights in the different types of aircraft was about an hour, more or less. All of the aircraft that were flying were listed on a chalkboard in the operations section of the school. You could look at the board and see which airplanes were flying and who was flying them.

On this particular day, as I was leaving operations for my flight in the P-63, I scanned the board to see which airplanes were flying and who was flying them. The B-17 was being flown by a couple of my good buddies, students of the school. I was cruising around in the P-63 and having a ball with the fighter airplane, and I saw the B-17 off in the distance. Since my buddies were flying it, I thought that I would have some fun and give them a thrill. One of the flaws of the P-63 was that it developed an aileron flutter at about 450 to 465 mph. I had tried it and, sure enough, it happened. (That is the reason that we gave most of those airplanes to the Russians.)

The B-17 was at about 6,000 or 7,000 feet so I climbed to about 10,000 and was quite a distance behind him. I dove toward him from above and to his rear and got the airplane up to about 450 mph and flew under the B-17. The cruising speed of the B-17 was around 155 mph so I was going a lot faster than he was when I passed under the airplane. As I got to the front part of the B-17 I pulled the P-63 up sharply. I zoomed up in front of the B-17 and barely missed contacting the #3 prop with the tail of my aircraft. I had not taken into consideration the fact that he was moving forward also, even though at a slower speed. It scared the hell out of me and I was sure that it scared my buddies in the B-17 to see an airplane zooming up right in front of them. I climbed up and turned away and headed back to the airfield. I was really shaken by my near-miss. My time was about up so I landed and taxied back to the school.

I climbed out of the airplane and walked into the operations office. I logged in and the aircraft was listed as available for the next flight. Lucky for me, one of the instructor pilots took the airplane for the next hour. As I scanned the board I noticed that my buddies were not the ones who were flying the B-17 when I buzzed it. The school commandant and a student were in the airplane. The crew was switched after I took off for my flight in the P-63. My heart sunk, I thought that I would be kicked out of the school and maybe court marshaled for the buzz job that I had given the B-17. I stood there in the operations office and waited my fate. The B-17 landed shortly afterward and the commandant came storming into operations. He said, "Who in hell is flying that P-63?" He looked at the board and saw that one of his instructors was flying the P-63 because he had taken the airplane as soon as I logged out of it. The commandant said, "Oh, never mind." I just stood there, trembling in my boots. I had just had another couple of very lucky thing happen to me. I had just missed killing myself with the zoom and now the commandant was blaming his instructor for the buzz job. I did not bravely step up and admit that it had been me flying the P-63 when the incident took place.

The Test Pilot School took about 3 ½ months and it was pretty intensive training we had a pretty good knowledge of the details of the various systems of all of the different aircraft as well as the ability to fly them. All of the time that I had been there I had been on TDY (temporary duty) from Wright Field. After I graduated from the school I hitched a ride on a military aircraft back to Wright Field and reported in. I went up to see the Colonel in Personnel who had sent me to the school and told him all about the school and my experiences while there. He told me that he had an assignment for me as a test pilot in the Mid-West Procurement District, which had its headquarters in Wichita, Kansas. I took a few days leave and went up to St. Marys to see my folks before I took off again. While I was up there I went car shopping. I figured I was going to need a car if I was going to Kansas, besides; it was time that I had a car again. I had not had one since I sold mine when I went into the Cadet program in 1942.

I managed to find a 1941 Dodge that was not all worn out. There were no new cars being produced in America. The last year of production had been in 1942. All used cars were at a premium. I think I paid about $1,200 for that Dodge. (Lucky me, I had won that much playing poker during the 7 months overseas.) It was a 2-door model, called a Club Coupe. I was able to get coupons for gasoline to make the trip since I was traveling on military orders. I got some pretty good recapped tires and off I went for Wichita. My belongings were minimal, so everything I owned fit into the car with ease.

Chapter 16
Test Pilot - Boeing - Wichita

I arrived at the Headquarters for Air Service Command Mid-Western Procurement District. It was located in a part of the building that served as the terminal for the Wichita Municipal Airport. I reported in and was being interviewed by the Commander of the District. He said that he had two openings for a test pilot; one was at the Convair factory in the Fort Worth, Texas area where they were making the monster aircraft, the B-36, and the other was right there in Wichita at the Boeing factory where they were making the B-29. I said that I would prefer to be flying the B-29 to the B-36 so I would like to stay in the Wichita area at the Boeing factory. He said, "Good, that is what I had in mind for you anyhow, since you have been flying Boeing B-17's." He said that after I got checked in I should go over to the Beech factory, which was on the other side of town and get checked out in the C-45. The Beech C-45 was a small passenger plane that could carry about 8 people. It was a twin-engine aircraft and had a pretty good cruising speed. I flew with the Air Force test pilot for a couple of days and was now checked out in the C-45.

When I first checked in at the headquarters I asked about housing and was told that there was a tight housing situation in Wichita because of all of the aircraft factory workers in town at the 4 different aircraft factories that were in the immediate area. There was the huge Boeing plant, Beech, Cessna and Culver, all of them producing aircraft for the war effort. One really nice lady in the personnel section told me that she knew of a family that would permit me to use an apartment in their basement until I could find a place to live. There was no military base there in Wichita, so we had to live on the economy just like a civilian. She also told me that there was a dance at one of the large hotels in Wichita that next Saturday night and that she wanted to introduce me to a really nice girl. I was all for that, so I told her that I would be there. That lady was really nice, she got me set up with a temporary apartment and was going to introduce me to a nice girl. She was also very pretty, but she was a married lady, so I just waited until Saturday night.

The first morning that I tried to go to work from my temporary basement apartment, my car was frozen up. There was some moisture in the fuel and it had frozen hard in the fuel filter. It was just one chunk of ice. It took me several hours to get the old Dodge running and then I knew enough to put some alcohol in the gas tank to prevent that from happening again. I came straggling into work at the Boeing factory really late, but with a good excuse.

There were only 6 test pilots there and every B-29 produced had to be flown by an Air Force test pilot before it could be accepted by the US Army Air Force. A couple of them had extensive additional duties and were only available to fly at selected times. There were 4 of us assigned to the operations section, so our primary duty was flying. We all had other duties around the factory. I became the Security Officer and was responsible for the security of the entire factory. It was really a token job, because the factory had a complete civilian security force, well organized and well manned. I was just a figurehead to show that the military was in charge of the security. I did go to the security meetings and got to know the supervisors of the sections.

I began flying B-29s right away, as co-pilot with the more experienced pilots. I was also studying the tech orders on the aircraft to familiarize myself with the systems. On the test flights, which generally took about two hours, we checked all the systems of the aircraft to make sure that they were working properly. Our crewmembers were all civilians except for the two pilots. They were civil service technicians and were experts in their field. We even had some female technicians who flew with us on our test flights. If there was a system that was not working properly we wrote up the discrepancy and it had to be fixed before we could accept the airplane. If the problem could be fixed and adequately checked out on the ground after the repair we may not have to fly the aircraft again, but some discrepancies required repair and another test flight before we could accept the airplane. I was checked out as first pilot in the B-29 a couple of months after I got there. We took turns flying the left seat on the test flights, although we had one pilot who never did check out as first pilot. He didn't really care.

Flying B-29 on Test Hop

I found a little one bedroom furnished apartment with a garage after a few days in the basement apartment and moved in. I was really living it up. I went to the dance and met the nice girl that I had been told about and we hit it off immediately. Her name was Tina Gilliland. I had arrived in Wichita in November of 1944 and in May of 1945 I changed her name to Tina Bushong. We were married on the 4th of May. My brother, Clyde, who was in the Navy, was being transferred from Norfolk, Virginia to Texas and we made all of the arrangements so he could be there and be the best man at our wedding. I had been the best man at his wedding, so it was really nice that he could be there to do that job for me.

The day of the big wedding, I flew a test flight and took my brother along. He got a kick out of seeing his little brother flying that big airplane and, of course, I had to show off a little.

Our wedding took place in the pastor's house in El Dorado, Kansas where Tina's mother and sister lived. It was only about 25 miles from Wichita. Tina and I went to Ohio for our honeymoon. Not a very romantic place, but I wanted my folks and Tina to meet. We spent a night or two in Chicago on the way and on the way back, so that was a little more romantic.

We found a little nicer one-bedroom apartment and moved. My job at the Boeing plant was great. It was about like a civilian job except that I did not get paid for the overtime that I put in and I had to wear a uniform to work.

The B-29s kept rolling off the assembly line and each one of them had to be flown by an Air Force test pilot. We had to have VFR (Visual Flight Rules) to perform the test flights, so we occasionally got behind when the weather was bad. One time we had over 1.2 miles of B-29s lined up, wingtip to wingtip, waiting to be test flown. I remember flying and accepting five in one day when the weather finally cleared. That was a long, hard day. When I came home that evening, I bragged to Tina about how much money I had spent that day. I had accepted five aircraft for the Army Air Force at a cost of $760,000 each. I was really spending the big bucks.

During the time that I was there, the factory produced five special airplanes. They all came down the assembly line together and were called "Project Silver Plate". We didn't know what was special about them, but we knew that they were different. During the production, a Lt. Colonel named Tibbets came in a couple of times to check on the aircraft. We later found out what he was up to when he dropped the bomb on Hiroshima. The five aircraft that were on our production line were part of his project, but none of them was the one that dropped the bomb.

When the war ended, the production line for the B-29s

stopped immediately. There was no further need to produce those airplanes. I received orders to transfer to McClellan AFB, near Sacramento California. That sounded great to me and Tina was also pleased, so we bundled everything that we owned into that 1941 Dodge Club Coupe and headed off for California.

I had never been to California, but Tina had been there several times. Her Grandmother, two uncles and several cousins lived in the center portion of the San Joaquin Valley. We planned our trip to go through the part of California where they lived. We visited a few days with her relatives and during that time she said that she wanted to introduce me to a cousin of hers who had flown B-17s in England during the war. We stopped at his mother's house in the little town of Chowchilla to find where we could locate him. His mother told us that he was building a house and how to get to where he was building it. We drove up in front of the house and her cousin walked around the corner of the house toward us. I said, "Hi, Mac." and he said, "Hi Red." I recognized him as the Donald McGregor who had been in the same squadron that I was with the 390th Bomb Group in England.

Our crews had gotten to the 390th at the same time and we buddied around with McGregor's crew a lot until they were transferred to the "Pathfinder Group". That was the one group of B-17s that was equipped with radar and was called upon to provide the lead aircraft when we were to bomb through the clouds. Their equipment could see the target on the radar and we would all drop our bombs when they dropped. The radar was pretty primitive, but it was the best we had at the time.

On one mission, Donald and his crew were coming to the 390th to be our lead aircraft. They were arriving at about 2:00 AM. Their aircraft had a load of bombs on board, but was not fully fueled. Donald turned on his landing lights on the final approach to the field and was shot down right there on the final approach by a German aircraft that just happened to be in the right spot at the right time. (Wrong spot and wrong time for Donald.)

Donald's aircraft crashed into the ground a couple of

miles from our airfield. Fortunately, for him and his crew, there were some English troops camped nearby. They ran out to the crashed aircraft and started dragging the crewmen out of the aircraft and into an area behind a stone wall nearby. The airplane blew up, but the crew was saved by the efforts of the English troops. Donald sustained serious injuries and was retired from the service on a physical disability. "Mac" and I had quite a chat and then Tina and I proceeded onward to Sacramento.

We arrived at Sacramento and I began my check-in procedures. This was the first time I had ever checked into a base as a married man. Always before, there had been some kind of quarters available for me as a single officer. Now things were quite different. There were no family quarters available on McClellan AFB. We checked into a motel and began to look for a place to rent. The manager of the motel said that he would only let us stay for five days. If we stayed longer than that, he would have to give us a weekly rate and he did not want to do that. It took several days for me to find out what I was going to be doing at McClellan. When I found out, I was very disappointed. My duty was to be as an administrative officer with duty in the separation center where they were processing men coming back from overseas for discharge. They said that they liked to have an officer with "lots of lettuce" signing the discharge papers. It made the men coming back from overseas feel better if the guy who signed their discharge had medals earned in combat.

That certainly didn't sound like good duty to me. I asked about flying and was told, "Oh, you will be able to get your 4 hours per month." I was used to flying almost every day and some days, lots of flying. That didn't sound good at all to me. As I was processing in, a WAF Lieutenant who was processing my papers said, "Wow, you have a lot of points, you could get out right now." (Points were awarded for combat, medals, overseas time and total time in service.) I said, "I can? Why don't you just hold my papers until tomorrow?" There were several things that made me feel that it would be a smart move to get out:

1. I was not thrilled with the duty that I would be having.

2. We could not find a place to live. We had already had to move to another motel.

3. I had asked for a few days leave to go back to Madera, California and go hunting with Tina's two uncles. They had told me when we came through there that they were going deer hunting and that I could go along with them if I could get leave. I had never been deer hunting and really wanted to go. I was told that I would be too busy signing discharge papers to take any leave time.

I came back to the motel and talked it over with Tina. She had never been around a military base and was thoroughly disgusted with our living situation, so she was all in favor of my getting out. I went back the next day and told the WAF to go ahead and process me out of the service. That may have been one of the dumbest moves I ever made, or maybe the smartest. I really don't know. Things worked out OK, so I guess it was not too bad a decision. Anyhow, the WAF did process me out of the service and during the processing; she asked me if I would like to stay in the Reserve forces. I said I would, so I was released from active duty as a 1st Lieutenant in the Army Air Force Reserve.

Tina and I headed back to Madera, California, and I went deer hunting with her two uncles. I got a deer, too, but that is a whole other story.

Chapter 17
Between Wars

We had no place to live there in Madera, but Tina had two uncles living there, so we stayed with them for a while. I had some terminal leave pay coming, about 2 months worth, and there was "mustering out pay" which was about $100 per month for 3 months. We were looking around for a house that we could afford and without a job we couldn't afford much. We found an old house in a good area of Madera and called Dad to see if he would put up the money. The house was only $3500.00. Dad sent the money and we bought the house. In the meantime I had started to draw a weekly amount from the employment office. The government had established a program for all returning veterans to draw a weekly sum of $20 until they could get established and find a job. We had to report to the local office of the California Employment Service each week and check for jobs and get our check. Well, the employment office was understaffed to take care of the workload of all the returning veterans and within a few weeks, both Tina and I were working there. I was a claims examiner and she was a secretary to the manager. We were doing pretty well and what a fine place to look for a job.

Jobs were scarce and housing was very limited. Things were beginning to get going after the country got started in the post war production. There had been so many items that were not manufactured during the war that there were severe shortages in lots of things. The housing industry began to try to fill the need for all the new families that had been created during the war. Many of the wives had continued living with their parents while their husbands were off fighting the war. Now they needed a house to live in as a family. No new cars had been produced for about four years and the old ones were giving out. It was amazing how many items we needed that had not been available during the war, shoes, tires, refrigerators and all kinds of appliances. Things were booming.

I finally got a job with the local Buick/GMC dealer as the parts department manager/trainee. It was training under the GI Bill. After months of training I was qualified as a journeyman parts department manager. Although automobiles were being produced, there were not enough to satisfy the demand, so cars sold at a premium and parts were in big demand to repair the old vehicles.

The armed services were decimated and the reserve forces were in a very disorganized state. Nothing was being done and it was nearly impossible to find anyone who knew anything about anything connected with the reserve forces. I finally found that there were meetings of the Army Air Force Reserves being held in Fresno, which was about 22 miles from Madera. I attended a few of them and everyone was totally confused. There was no organization and no plan for training. I made sure that I was signed in at all of the meetings that I attended so I would at least get credit for being there. There were a couple of years of disorganization before we really got organized.

In the meantime, I had found that Lieutenants with less time in grade than I had when I got out had been promoted to Captain in the reserve when they were released from active duty. I wondered why I had not been promoted. I requested copies of my OERs (Officer Effectiveness Report) and I found that one report for a 60 day period in England was slightly below the norm. A Major Armstrong, who was the Squadron Commander of the 569th Bomb Squadron that I had been assigned to in the 390th Bomb Group, made the rating. During the time covered by the report I had flown several practice missions and several combat missions and had been in the hospital for 30 days of the 60 days that the report covered. During that period I had never met my commanding officer and I was sure that he had no idea who I was. I composed a long letter explaining the circumstances and sent it to the Adjutant General of the U.S. Army and requested that the subject OER be removed from my file and that I be promoted to Captain in the Army Air Force Reserve. It happened. The file was removed and shortly after that I received my promotion to Captain.

It was interesting that my brother, who was a Chief Petty Officer in the Navy when the war started, was commissioned and had been promoted to Lieutenant in the Navy prior to my promotion. He chided me slightly about being ahead of me, because a Lieutenant in the Navy is equivalent to a Captain in the Army. I chided him right back, saying that I would bet that I would make Captain before he did. A Captain in the Navy is equivalent of a full Colonel in the Air Force. Of course, when I made Captain, he again rubbed it in saying that he was getting paid for his rank. He was still on active duty. He retired as a Commander, after 28 years of continuous service.

Chapter 18
Recalled to active duty - Alaska

The Reserve Forces finally got organized and I was assigned to Castle Army Air Force Base for reserve training. I had a spot in the organization and went there for a day each month for training. About that time the Air Force became a separate service. So we had to buy new uniforms and we became black shoe pilots instead of brown shoe pilots. We still did the same jobs and the airplanes still flew just like they did before. I had what they called an M-Day Assignment at Castle. The M stood for Mobilization so that when we mobilized I had a spot to fill and since I had that tag of "Flight Test Officer"; I was naturally assigned to the Flight Test section.

The aircraft that were assigned to Castle Air Force Base were B-50's and B-29's. Since I had quite a bit of B-29 time, I had no problem with that airplane. The ones that were assigned there had been converted to tankers for in-flight refueling, so they were a different configuration than the ones I had flown at the factory. They flew about the same, but I had to learn about the refueling system. The B-50's were somewhat similar to the B-29's, but had more powerful engines and more advanced systems, so I had to go to school to learn those systems.

I went up to Castle AFB once a month and did my training. I got to fly some each time I went up there, so I was not too far from being proficient. Our reserve training days were paid days so the extra income was pretty handy too. Things went along like that until 1951 when the Korean War started. Then they changed IN A BIG WAY.

The people with the M-Day assignments were recalled to active duty. The Air Force grew very quickly to support the war effort in Korea. I was recalled to active duty at Castle AFB in June of 1951. Naturally, I was assigned to the Flight Test Section. There were several officers from the town of Madera, where Tina and I were living, who were recalled at that time. We drove back and forth together and continued to live in Madera for a time. Gradually, our group from Madera diminished as we received assignments to other bases.

Not long after my recall to active duty, our first child, Richard, Jr. was born. We were so proud of him and so glad to have him. We had been married six years by the time he came along. He was born in Madera, California where we had lived during the time between wars.

The Maintenance Control Officer decided that I needed to have some additional training in the Aircraft Maintenance Management area so he had me sent back to Chanute AFB in Illinois for a six-week course. Tina and the new baby went along. Housing was very hard to find and we finally settled for a two-room apartment in a sort of disreputable part of Rantoul, Illinois. It was OK for the six weeks that we were there. My classes were from 6:00 AM until noon and then study and writing into the evening. It turned winter while we were there and it was no fun getting to school by 0600.

Upon my return to Castle AFB from the temporary duty at Chanute AFB, I learned that I had been on orders to ship out to Korea. My departure date was to have been a couple of days after I got back from the school. My boss went storming up to the personnel office and told them to put someone else on those orders to Korea. He said that it would be completely unfair to send me over there immediately after getting back from TDY (temporary duty). WOW, was I glad that he did that.

The handwriting was on the wall, though. I was going overseas and soon.

Shortly after that, the personnel officer called me and told me that there was an opening for an officer of my rank and qualifications at Elmendorf AFB near Anchorage, Alaska. I didn't have to think about it twice. It sounded so much better than Korea that I jumped at the chance. So off I went to Alaska. Tina could not go until I had found suitable family housing, and that was not easy.

I arrived up there in May of 1952. It took a while to get the car shipped up, but Major Bud Grey, whom I had bunked with on the ship enroute to Alaska, had a friend who loaned us a car to go house hunting. Housing was really tight and Major Grey and I ended up buying a duplex together. It was not quite finished, but we could handle the completion and it was quite nice housing. It was small, just two bedrooms on each side and very small rooms, but it was cozy and considered adequate housing, so our families could now come up to Alaska.

My first assignment was to the flight test section as a test pilot, but that didn't last long. Since I had graduated from the test pilot school, I was considered a fully qualified aircraft maintenance officer. All of the studying that we did in the test pilot school taught us pretty much how all the systems on all aircraft operated. So I quickly was assigned as OIC (Officer in Charge) of the Field Maintenance Shops and hanger. We did fairly major maintenance on all kinds of aircraft. I had about 75 to 80 personnel working for me at that time. I enjoyed that job and got to do quite a bit of flying into some pretty wild places.

After about a year in that job I was called to report to the Commander of the Air Force Depot for Alaska. He was a full Colonel and I reported to him and he asked me if I thought I could handle the job as Chief of the Depot Shops. It was a job calling for a Lt. Colonel and I was still just a lowly Captain. I jumped at the chance and that was my job for the rest of the time I was in Alaska. In that job, I had about 900 people, GI's and civilians under my supervision. I appreciated the opportunity to perform in a job like that one.

In the meantime, our second child, Rebecca, was born. She was born in the hospital at Fort Richardson, which was near Elmendorf. Alaska was still a territory at that time. She was born in April of 1953 and the roads were still covered with ice and snow. Fort Richardson was several miles from our little duplex. I drove as rapidly as I could, under the slick conditions, to get Tina to the hospital before the baby arrived. We made it OK and Rebecca arrived on schedule.

That event occurred just nine months and one week after Tina arrived in Alaska. We knew that it was not the long winter nights in Alaska that brought about the crop of babies, but the long summer days. It didn't even get dark at night at the time that Tina arrived. At midnight it was just like dusk. I sat in our living room at midnight one night, and read a news paper without any lights turned on, just so I could say that I had done it.

Where we were, just outside of Anchorage, was quite different than farther north. At Ladd AFB, near Fairbanks, they used to play a baseball game at midnight on the 4th of July without lights.

We moved into base housing shortly after Rebecca was born. We enjoyed our tour in Alaska. It was designated as a two-year tour, but we liked it so much that I extended our tour for another year. We got to move into newly constructed base housing for that last year. It was quite nice, with three bedrooms upstairs and a full basement below. I put some swings in the basement for the kids and we made a playroom for them there. It was too cold for them to play outside very much.

All the time that we lived in Alaska, we never had a garage. Our car sat out and needed special care so it would start when we wanted to use it. I had a special head bolt installed in the engine, which was an electric heater. I plugged it into the house electric system at night and the engine was warm enough to start in the morning. I had to do some special things with the tires also. Tubeless tires would freeze so hard that they would break and develop leaks, so I had to install tubes in them.

In addition to my duties as OIC of the Depot Shops, I flew a lot, every chance I got. I was checked out in the C-47, which we called the "Gooney Bird". It was the old Douglas DC-3. We used it for carrying cargo and passengers to some really weird places, the remote radar sites that we had all over Alaska to watch the Russians when they flew. Anything that headed toward the US was suspect and fighter aircraft would be scrambled if they got too close. We were in the Korean War at that time, which was being supported by Russia, and there was a great fear that the Russians would attack us. Those radar sites were really remote. They built some of them right where they could drop a bulldozer to begin construction. The runways were very short and built on hillsides. That was some scary flying. The weather that we flew in was severe. We carried survival gear with us on every flight in case we went down in the wilderness.

I also got to fly quite a bit in a real bush plane. It was the DeHavalin Beaver, a single engine, high wing airplane that could get into and out of very short strips. It could carry quite a bit of cargo or five passengers. It was a very versatile aircraft and a lot of fun to fly. I got down and buzzed moose and Kodiak bears with that airplane.

As our three years came to an end, we were permitted to request the area that we wished to be assigned for our next tour. I asked for SOUTH east or SOUTH west. I really wanted to go somewhere that was warm after three years in Alaska. When my assignment came through it was to Cape Cod, Massachusetts. I figured that the only place that was south of was Alaska. My assignment was as a pilot though and I thought that would be great. I had been an Aircraft Maintenance Officer for the previous three years and now I was just going to be a pilot. I thought, how nice, I'll probably just fly every three days or so and I'll be able to get a boat and go fishing and spend a lot of time with the family.

We took a few weeks leave on the way to Massachusetts. We came down by ship, which was quite an adventure. None of us got seasick, but there were a lot of others who did. We picked up a new Buick in Seattle and started for California. My folks lived in Madera and we had a nice visit with them and stopped along the way to Cape Cod to visit my sister and brother and Tina's sister and brothers. We saw a good part of the country on that trip.

Our two children did not know what hot weather was. As we were driving across the desert it was up to 120 degrees and our new car had no air conditioner. Air conditioners were not very popular at that time, just beginning to show up in cars.

Becky thought that she was cold and wanted to put a coat on. She thought that more clothes took care of any uncomfortable feeling. She had lived in Alaska all of her life up to that point.

Chapter 19
Cape Cod - Cold War - Colorado Springs

We arrived at Otis AFB on Cape Cod and, as I started to check into the squadron that I had been assigned to as a pilot, I was told to report to the commander of the Aircraft Maintenance Squadron. I reported in to him and he rubbed his hands with glee. He said, "This wing is just forming and just beginning to get our aircraft and we do not have any qualified Aircraft Maintenance Officers. You are IT." There I was again, a fully qualified maintenance officer and with three years of experience in Alaska. I was the first maintenance officer and we had very few maintenance personnel, very little equipment, and no hangers. It was a mess. We were way behind where we should be and getting new airplanes every few days. The airplanes were the RC-121's. They were a complete airborne radar station with the capability to detect any incoming aircraft and scramble fighters from the ground and direct the fighters during the attack on the enemy aircraft. They were very complicated, quite sophisticated for their time and there we were, not prepared to maintain them.

Housing was at a premium in the area around the base. There was very little base housing and it was all occupied. We had to look on the civilian economy for housing. We finally found a house in North Falmouth. It was not very far from the base and was a pretty nice house, but it had been intended as a summer home and was a big rambling house with little, if any, insulation. It belonged to one of the Rand girls (of the Remington-Rand family). Mr. Rand had built a summer home for himself and one for each of his daughters in the same area of North Falmouth. They were all big homes intended for summer entertainment. Ours was four bedrooms upstairs, a large dining room and a big living room with a huge fireplace.

There was a large buffalo head mounted and hung on the

wall facing you as you came down the stairway. The kids were scared of it at first. We survived for the first winter there, and then moved to Sandwich while base housing was being constructed. One of the houses that we rented in Sandwich was on a hill overlooking Cape Cod Bay. It was on a 14-acre lot and I could have bought it for $28,000. (This was not the first or last mistake that I ever made, but one of the biggest ones. We are thinking well over a million dollars for those 14 acres today.)

After that first year, we also had hangers for maintaining our large fleet of RC-121 aircraft. They had continued to arrive and we had our full complement by the end of the year. The first year was tough though. We were training our maintenance personnel, getting our equipment and new aircraft and trying to keep the aircraft flying. We were in the middle of a "Cold War". We expected the Russians to launch an attack on us at any time and our job was to get those aircraft flying so we could have four of them continuously on station about 400 miles out over the Atlantic as airborne radar stations.

The mission was to have four aircraft on station 24 hours a day and every day of the year. The radar crews aboard the aircraft were monitoring every airborne object that was headed toward the United States. The stations that were manned by the aircraft were spaced so that the radar capability of each station overlapped the capability of the neighboring station. It was a terrific job for the maintenance crews to keep launching an aircraft every two hours to replace the ones that were on station. The station time scheduled for each aircraft was eight hours and it was a couple of hours out to the station and a couple of hours back home, so the mission was scheduled as a 12 hour mission. Any delay of the next aircraft in arriving on station would delay the departure of the aircraft on station. Weather was critical and could delay departures and returns. At times we had aircraft all over the place because of weather at the home base. Our primary alternate air base was Bermuda. If the weather was below landing minimums at Otis AFB, our aircraft were diverted to Bermuda. The crew would be allowed 24 hours of crew rest and then fly another mission on the way home.

After we got enough maintenance personnel and got them trained and also got equipment to maintain the aircraft, the operation ran pretty smoothly. Of course, the aircrews were also in an intense training program. All the pilots had to be checked out on the RC-121. No one who was assigned had ever flown one before. As soon as I could, I got into the training program as a pilot. I had to do that in addition to my job as aircraft maintenance officer. I wanted to fly the aircraft and the ground study for getting checked out as a pilot got me better acquainted with all systems of the aircraft so I could talk more intelligently to the maintenance personnel about the aircraft repair.

The first time I climbed into the aircraft with an instructor pilot, he turned to me and asked, "How old are you?" I told him I was 32 years old. He said, "OK, you are eligible to fly this airplane. We just do not check anybody out in the airplane who is over 40 years old." I asked him why the restriction on age existed. He said, "Because no one over 40 can stand three pieces of tail this close together." (If you remember, the Constellation aircraft had three tails and the RC-121 was a stretched version of the Constellation.) It was an on-going joke about the three tails.

RC-121 D -- The Three Tail Constellation

After all of our aircraft had arrived and our maintenance personnel were pretty well trained on the aircraft it became an almost routine, but tedious job. I worked 6 days and then had two days off and changed shift. We had to have a maintenance officer on duty every hour of every day. I was trying to fly a mission as Aircraft Commander on my days off, so I was gone from home a lot. We finally got quarters on base and that made things a little easier for Tina and for me.

About that time I decided that I should apply for a regular commission in the Air Force. I did not have a college degree, but I had taken college courses along the way every chance that I got. There was an integration program going on at that time, so there was a chance for me to get a regular commission, a slim chance but.... what do you know, I got the regular commission. I was competing with officers who had multiple degrees and it was a pleasant surprise when I received word that I had made it. On the next promotion cycle after I got the regular commission, I was promoted to Major, another pleasant surprise.

Lots of things happened at Otis and the years flew by. About four years after we were assigned there I was transferred to Headquarters Air Defense Command at Colorado Springs. I was to be in the Maintenance Directorate and would be the specialist for the RC-121 aircraft. There were two wings of those aircraft by that time, one on each coast. The west coast wing was stationed at McClelland AFB near Sacramento, California and had similar duties, four radar stations off the coast as Airborne Early Warning and Control. I quickly picked up responsibility for several other aircraft in the Maintenance Directorate, but my primary responsibility for the first two years there was the RC-121 fleet. I had to do a lot of traveling to tend to provisioning and maintenance problems and I was a member of the Inspector General Team for performing Operational Readiness Inspections on each wing.

On one occasion while I was stationed at the Headquarters, I was the maintenance member of an Inspector General (IG) team that performed an Operational Readiness Inspection (ORI) on the Airborne Early Warning and Control Wing on the West coast (McClelland AFB). I kept warning the Maintenance Control Officer that his readiness was not meeting the specifications and that he would fail the inspection if he did not bring the number of aircraft that were operationally ready up to the standards. He didn't and I failed him. That was a big deal to fail a portion of an ORI. The bad thing about failing him was that much later, when I was in Japan, he came in as the maintenance member of the ORI team in the Far Eastern Command to give our wing an Operational Readiness Inspection. He gave me a sadistic smile as we met when the team arrived. The good news was that he could not find anything to fail my portion of the maintenance operation.

After a couple of years in ADC Headquarters I was moved to the job of Assistant to the Chief of the Maintenance Division. One of my jobs was to brief the three star General who was in charge of the Logistics for the Air Defense Command. I did this with "flip-charts" that I made on butcher paper. (Today those briefings would be done with a laptop computer and screen projector.) One day, as I reported in to the General's office for the briefing, he said, "You are Major Bouchard aren't you?" I replied, "No sir, I am Major Bushong. Major Bouchard gets credit for everything I do and I get blamed for everything that he does." Bouchard was a good friend of mine and worked in the same directorate. I meant my remarks as a joke and the general took them that way, but he never forgot my name after that.

The Cuban Crisis occurred during my third year at the Headquarters. I was in my office, at the desk next to the Chief of the Maintenance Section, when an officer from the head of the Logistics came in and said for me to come with him. I went, but my boss was looking at him and me questioningly. I was taken to a room within a room with all the doors closed and briefed on what was going on. I was told to tell no one, not even my boss. I was to be on a team to be responsible for the movement of aircraft and munitions into a position to defend the southeastern portion of the United States and be prepared to move several squadrons of RC-121 aircraft into that area for radar protection and control of fighters. It appeared that we were going to war over the Cuban crisis.

After my briefing I went back to my office and sat down

and my boss said, "What was that all about?" I answered him saying, "I can't tell you." As you might imagine, that went over like a lead balloon. He ranted and raved for a while and then gave up. Shortly after that they came and got me again for more briefing. I was to run a command post all of that night. I would be by myself and responsible for movement of aircraft and munitions into the southeastern states all night long. Most of the traffic was going into Florida. I was afraid that Florida might sink from the amount of equipment that we moved into there that night.

The next day was Saturday and we had promised to go to the dedication game at the new Air Force Academy Stadium with the Bouchards. I got a couple of hours sleep after I was relieved at the command post and we went to the game. Of course I couldn't tell Tina or the Bouchards what was going on. Chuck Bouchard asked me what I had been doing the night before and when I said, "I can't tell you", he asked no more.

In the middle of the game there was an announcement over the PA system: "All medical personnel, report to the front ticket booth." I was sure that the war had started. I waited for pandemonium to take over the whole stadium. Nothing happened! I never did find out why all the medical personnel had to report.

After the game, the Bouchards came to our house for dinner. We were sitting around having an after-dinner drink and I could hardly hold my eyes open because of being up all night the night before, when the phone rang. It was a Colonel from the Logistics Directorate. He said, "Pack your bag and be at Peterson Field at 10:00 tonight." I said, "What kind of clothes will I need, cold weather or warm weather?" He laughed and said, "Take your choice." My hunch was that I was going someplace where it was warm after sending all those airplanes and munitions down to Florida during the night before.

I went back into the living room and told the Bouchards that I was sorry, but I had some things to do. Chuck's eyebrows rose a little, but he knew better than to ask questions. They left quickly and I started to pack. Tina wanted to know where I was going and I told her that I could not tell her. She had been around the Air Force long enough to not ask questions. She just helped me pack. I was a quick packer since I traveled so much.

I reported out to the airport a little early and there were several officers there, waiting. I knew most of them, although they were from different Directorates all over the Headquarters. We were not told where we were going. There was a Colonel in charge of the group of eight officers. We piled on the aircraft and took off. I got a little sleep on the aircraft and I suppose everyone else did also. We arrived in Louisiana at just before daylight and we all went into the blockhouse that was the control center for the Air Defense Sector of the South Eastern United States.

We reported in to the Commander of the Sector, who was a Major General. He was really haggard looking and bleary-eyed. I guessed that he had not had much sleep in the past few days. His first question, after we reported in, was; "Are you here to augment my staff?" The Colonel with us said, "No, General, but we are here to help you in any way we can." He introduced us all and told the General what our specialties were and we were spread around amongst the staff of the Sector.

The blockhouse had no windows and we became very busy coordinating the needs of the sector with the headquarters. Each of us had contacts back at the headquarters who could make things happen in a hurry. We were amassing fighters in that area, preparing for an assault by the Cubans at any minute. I coordinated the movement of a squadron of the RC-121 aircraft to Florida with flight crews, maintenance crews and all of the equipment that they would need to operate for an indefinite period. They were sent to Orlando. They could fly radar patrol off the coast and give advance warning of any aircraft approaching the US. They could also control fighters to intercept any aircraft that was headed toward our country. We worked through the day and way into the next night before we left the blockhouse. We were beat and so was the regular staff of the Sector, but they were now in a better position to defend the US.

One thing that we ran up against was that none of our fighter aircraft had a machine gun. It was antiquated, but so were the aircraft that the Cubans might use to attack us. Our fighters had heat-seeking missiles and radar controlled missiles. The Cubans had aircraft similar to our B-26 medium range bomber that we had used in WWII. The heat-seeking missiles that we had on our fighter aircraft would be ineffective against that type of aircraft. One expression that I heard during that time was, "Couldn't I have just one little gun?" Later models of fighter aircraft were equipped with the Gattling gun which was a multi-barrel machine gun with a tremendous rate of fire and 20 to 30 MM projectiles, a very effective weapon.

After a little rest we went back into the blockhouse and helped the staff some more. Things had calmed down a little and it looked as though the anticipated war was not nearly as imminent. The next day we piled into our aircraft and flew back to Colorado Springs. My boss was really perturbed because he had not been informed of what I was doing. He got over it. I thought that we were into a war for sure during those three days. I remember telling Tina to get a stock of food and water and put them in our basement. I couldn't tell her what I was doing, but I wanted her and the kids to be prepared if we got into a war.

We were located very close to the Headquarters for NORAD (North American Air Defense Command). They were constructing the headquarters under Cheyenne Mountain, nearby, but did not have it completed yet, so the NORAD was located in buildings near our Headquarters. The Center being constructed under Cheyenne Mountain was to provide them with shelter and operational capability in case of nuclear attack. We were all thinking that a nuclear attack was very possible and one of the prime targets would be the NORAD Headquarters. If the enemy hit them with an atomic weapon, we would be right in the area of destruction.

As my tour at Headquarters ADC neared completion, I kept in pretty close contact with the officer in the Personnel section to try to get a good job for my next assignment. One day he called me and said the he had a great assignment and that I seemed to fit all the requirements except for one. The assignment was as "Air Attaché" to the Ambassador to Italy. The one qualification that he was not sure about was, "Did I speak Italian?" I immediately answered, "Si, spaghetti, macaroni and what else do you want to hear?" I meant it as a joke and he took it that way. He laughed and said, "Too bad, that would have been a wonderful assignment, and you fit the bill perfectly except for the language."

The next one he called about was an assignment to Yokota AFB in Japan. I checked out everything that I could to get information about the base (there was no internet in those days) and it sounded like a good assignment. Tina and I talked it over and thought it would be a great adventure for the entire family. Our kids were old enough that they would be able to enjoy all of the thrills of living in a foreign country, Rich was 12 and Beckie was 10. I accepted the assignment. It was not yet the end of the school year, so we had to get some special tests for the kids so that they could be given credit for finishing the grade that they were just about completing. Their teachers were cooperative and we got that done. We also had to sell our house. We got all of that done and our household goods crated for shipment and took a leave to go to California and visit my folks before our departure. We also shipped our car while we were in California so it would arrive in Japan shortly after we got there. There were thousands of details that had to be taken care of for an overseas shipment, but the standard procedures that the Air Force had established made it all pretty easy.

We spent some time with my parents, knowing that we would not see them again for at least three years. When the time came for our departure, Dad drove us up to Travis AFB and off we went.

Chapter 20
Yokota AFB, Japan

We were flying in a Military Air Transport (MATS) DC-6, a prop driven, pressurized passenger aircraft. Our first stop was Hickam AFB in Hawaii and it was late in the evening when we got there. Since we did not know if we would ever get there again, I got a cab and told the driver to take us all around to the places of interest on that island. We got about a three-hour ride, with numerous stops so we could see some of the sights of Honolulu. We even took a walk on Waikiki Beach in the darkness. It was the first time there for us.

We got back on our DC-6 and headed onward. Our next stop was Guam. It was hot and muggy there and, as we started to depart, the pressurization system in the aircraft failed. That meant that we would have to fly the rest of the way at low altitude. That would have been no big problem except that the air conditioning system was also failed. We were all hot and sweaty the rest of the way into Japan, it was a miserable flight. We landed about 8 PM, Japan time, but our minds and bodies thought it was about 4 AM and that we had missed the whole night's sleep.

The Air Force had a nice system to help an arriving officer and his family find their way around and get settled. There was a sponsor assigned to meet the aircraft and get us settled. Our sponsor was Captain Brown, who was going to be working for me, so we got special care. He and his wife met us in their air conditioned Cadillac and air conditioning never felt any better. They took us to the Officers Club for a late dinner and both of our kids fell asleep at the table. They had arranged for rooms for us at the base guest house, which was kind of like a motel. We went into our rooms and fell into bed. Well, about 3:00 AM we all woke up because it was way past our normal get-up time in the States. We prowled around the room and all tried to go back to sleep, but we were wide awake.

I checked into the base and into my job, which was Officer in Charge (OIC) of the Wing Quality Control Section. I was in charge of all of the inspectors who specialized in the aircraft and associated areas of maintenance. The Flight Test Section also came under my area of responsibility and Captain Brown was the chief Flight Test Officer. Everyone, including my boss, who was the Chief of Maintenance, understood that my first priority was to find a place for my family to live and get them settled and then I could go to work.

It rained and rained after we arrived in Japan. My shoes were soggy and the humidity was so high that they didn't dry out. I asked a young Japanese boy who worked at the guest house when the rainy season stopped. He said, "Oh, the rainy season has not started yet. It starts in two weeks." I wondered what was going to happen when the rainy season really got going, because it had rained every day since we had arrived. We found out that the Japanese had very strict time for each season to start and it didn't make any difference what nature wanted to do. For example, the cherry blossom festival was held at a certain time of the year and the cherry blossoms didn't always cooperate and bloom on that date.

One of the first priorities in the check-in was for Tina and me to go to school and get a drivers license for driving in Japan. They drive on the left side of the road and we had to learn the different signs and how to negotiate on the "wrong" side of the road. Captain Brown loaned us a small Japanese car to begin our search for housing. Base housing would not be available for about a year so we had to find something to rent or buy. There was a Johnson Air Force Base about eight miles from Yokota AFB where I was going to be working. We looked around there for housing that we could buy and there were several available, but we didn't like them so we started looking around the Yokota area. The homes that were bought by the American service men were called "paddy houses" because the land that they were built on was, in many cases, formerly a rice paddy. We found a house through word of mouth. Many people had been looking for a place for us. There was one that had just been vacated. It suited our needs so we bought it. It was adjacent to a housing area that was part of Yokota AFB.

The home was four bedrooms and two baths. It was on Japanese land and the land had a 20-year lease on it, 4 years of the land lease had been used, so there were 16 years left. The home was built by Japanese, supposedly to American standards, but it was far from the standards that we were used to. I had to duck to go through every door. We paid $5,000.00 for the house. We then started to get it ready to live in. We bought four used window air conditioners, had it painted, inside and out and had custom drapes made for the whole house, all the above work was done by Japanese for about $500.00, including the materials. After we moved in we had a bamboo fence built around our small yard, had a two-car carport built and lots more cabinets built into our kitchen area (another $400). It turned into a pretty comfortable house.

The fourth bedroom was in a separate wing of the house, designed as servant's quarters, and we hired a live-in maid for $30.00 a month and was she a dandy. When I got up at 5 AM each workday, I heard her stirring around and by the time I finished my shower, she had breakfast ready.

My job as OIC (Officer-in-Charge) of Wing Quality Control was a very interesting job. I quickly got into every area of the aircraft and equipment maintenance complex of the wing to find out what was going on and familiarize myself with the maintenance effort. There were about 1,800 people involved in the maintenance effort. One of the maintenance squadrons had quite a few Japanese technicians employed who worked along with the military specialists. The Japanese were excellent workmen and many were highly skilled in their specialties.

The wing was equipped with B-57's, Canberras, which had a nuclear delivery capability, but we were not prepared to deliver nukes from Japan. That was still a sensitive subject in Japan. The B-57's were pretty old airplanes at that time and there were much better ones in the inventory, but the wing was making do with what they had. I flew on several test flights with Captain Brown and it was a pretty nice airplane to fly. The dive-toss maneuver was part of the test flight. The airplane dove and released the bomb as it was pulling out of the dive and the airplane continued up and over to be headed the opposite direction to get away from the bomb blast. It was kind of a dive and half loop with a roll over at the top of the half loop.

Shortly after we got settled into our house an officer came by one evening and asked if I would participate in a Japanese/American Friendship golf tournament. I was delighted to be invited and agreed to participate. We were told where to be on what day and I was there. The tournament was on a Japanese course and two Americans were paired with two Japanese. By that time I had picked up a few words of Japanese and our Japanese partners had a little English, so we got along fine. The other American in the foursome was my boss, the Chief of Maintenance of the Wing. One of our Japanese partners was Nobuchika Yoshihara. He said to call him Jack. We had a great time on our way around the golf course and by the time we finished we were great friends with Jack Yoshihara. He invited us and our wives to come to his house for dinner that evening. He lived in the city of Ome`, which was about 20 miles from Yokota AFB.

Charlie Coffman, my boss, lived on base and therefore had a telephone. He called his wife and told her that we were going to Yoshihara's house for dinner and asked if she would go out to our house and tell Tina to get ready to go also. We didn't have a phone in our paddy house. Jack told us in detail how to get to his house and we all arrived on schedule. It was our first experience in a Japanese home and we were excited.

Jack and his wife met us at the front door and welcomed us to his home. We removed our shoes at the door and they were left in the entry-way. (I later found out that if your shoes were not turned around to point outward while you were in the house, you were not welcome back.) We were taken to Jack's entertainment room, which was also their bedroom. The bed was rolled up and in a closet. The floor of the room was covered with tatami mats which were woven grass and really pretty. All of the measurements in a Japanese home were made so that a certain number of tatami mats fit into each room.

The seating was on a cushion on the floor around the table, which was only about a foot from the floor. The room was very nice and had an alcove where there was a display that we were informed was changed with the seasons. There was also a beautiful Samurai sword on display in the alcove. The sliding door into the room was covered with rice paper. The hallway around the outer edge of the house was beautiful polished wood. It all was very impressive as Tina's and my first experience with a real Japanese home.

Mrs. Yoshihara did not join us in the room, but she brought all the refreshments and food to the door of the room. While she was in the hallway, outside the door, she got onto her knees and slid the door back and came into the room on her knees with the trays. She brought beer, sake and sushi (beautifully arranged). Then she later brought a gas burner and the ingredients for sukiyaki, which Jack cooked for us. Each time she came to the door she got down on her knees and entered the room on her knees. She spoke a little English and we could converse with her a bit. Jack's English was meager, but we were able to carry on a conversation, at least some conversation.

I admired Jack's samurai sword and he took it out of the scabbard and showed it to us. It was beautiful. From the pigeon English conversation about it, we were able to figure out that it was very old. Our evening was a tremendous success. Different from anything Tina and I had experienced, and although the Coffmans had been in Japan for a couple of years, I think it was a unique experience for them too. I told Jack where we lived and he was familiar with the paddy house section where our house was located.

The next evening Jack showed up at the base gate and they called me to get permission to let him in to the housing area that was adjacent to our group of paddy houses. To get to our house one had to come through part of the base housing section and then through a gate, which had been cut into the base fence to allow entry into our little group of houses. I had to go down the gate and lead Jack back to our house. When we got there he came in with a Samurai sword as a "presento" for me. It was a beautiful blade and he said, "If you ever need money take to hock shop, get takusan okani (lots of money). I was reluctant to take such a valuable sword as a present, but he insisted. I later got the history on the blade and found that it was made by a famous sword maker named Yosihira in the period around 1770. I still have it, and he was right, it is worth takusan okani.

I later got Jack a pass for his car so he could drive through the gate and come to our house. We had many wonderful and interesting experiences with our new Japanese friend, Nobuchika Yoshihara. I will tell you a few of them, but there were so many that I could fill a book just on our relation with Jack.

One evening, after I had gotten a pass for Jack's car, he appeared in front of our house in his Nissan Cedrick (the top of the line for Nissan, at that time). He got out of the driver's seat and went around to the trunk of his car and opened it. Out popped two geisha girls. I said, "Jack, why did you put them in the trunk?" He said, "I didn't think the guards would let me through the gate with geishas in the car." We took them into the house and had quite an evening with them and Jack. The geisha girls played games with the children and us. We chuckled about the girls in the trunk for a long time afterward.

I went trout fishing with Jack on a beautiful stream that was planted with trout every day. There was a charge to fish the stream and you paid by the weight for the trout that you caught. I caught several and we stopped by Jack's house after fishing and his wife cooked one for us. Jack had gone back into the woods near the stream and had come out with a radish that was kind of like horseradish. He took it home and his wife grated it and we used it for seasoning on the trout. I took one large trout home with me and wrapped it and put it into our freezer. Every time after that when Jack would come to our house with Japanese guests, he would go to the freezer and get that trout out and bang it on the table to show them how the silly Americans kept their fish.

Jack was a good friend and we enjoyed him and his family tremendously. He has visited us in the US several times and it was always a fun experience.

Chapter 21
Japan - Viet Nam

The Viet Nam conflict was just getting going and our whole wing of B-57's was sent to the Philippines to fly bombing missions in Viet Nam. Captain Brown went with the Wing on temporary duty. He had a small Honda motorcycle that he took with him so he would have transportation while down there. He had only been there a short time and, one evening, he had chained the front wheel of his motorcycle to a telephone post in front of his barracks, as he did every evening. When he came out the next morning, the front wheel was there, but the rest of the motorcycle was gone. Stealing was a way of life for the Filipinos.

Shortly after the B-57's left, the wing was equipped with F-105's. These were more modern aircraft, capable of supersonic speeds and equipped with the 20MM Gattling gun. They could carry more bombs on this single engine, single seat fighter aircraft than we could carry in the B-17 in our operation over Germany. The F-105 was also capable of delivering a nuclear weapon.

Our involvement in the Viet Nam conflict was being continually escalated. Our F-105 Wing finally deployed to Thailand and from there, flew combat missions into North Viet Nam. The name of the F-105 aircraft was "Thunderchief", and the nickname for it was "Thud" and so many of them were shot down in one area of North Viet Nam that the ridge was called "Thud Ridge". The 105 was a great airplane, but the North Vietnamese were being supplied with surface-to-air missiles (SAM) by the Russians. The SAMs were devastating to our effort. There was also anti-aircraft weaponry and even small arms fire caused aircraft damage. Back in Japan we were still doing major maintenance on the F-105 aircraft and equipment and I remember getting one engine back for maintenance that had been damaged in the compressor section by rifle fire.

After about a year as Chief of the Quality Control Section, I was assigned as OIC (officer in charge) of the entire shop section of the Field Maintenance Squadron. We were responsible for the maintenance of the sheet metal of the aircraft, the hydraulic systems, the engines, the fuel systems, all major systems of the aircraft except the electronics and the armament. I had almost 1,000 military specialists and 125 Japanese working for me. It was a great job and I spent a lot of hours getting up to speed on each of the special fields of maintenance. I had a familiarity with all of the shops from my duties as Quality Control Officer, but my new job required me to become more knowledgeable because I was supervising some highly qualified personnel.

My flying during the early time in Japan was the C-54, an old four engine transport, but reliable and able to carry supplies to all parts of Southeast Asia. I got to go on some pretty good trips on that old airplane. One trip, which I flew a few times, was a five-day trip out of Japan. We landed in Taiwan the first night at either Tainan or Taipei and spent the night there. The next day we would land at Clark field, in the Philippines, and then go into Manila and spend the night there. The next day we would go into Viet Nam, and leave there to spend the night in Bangkok, Thailand. We would then go into Hong Kong for two days and then back home. It was a great trip! We were delivering "precision measuring equipment" and picking up equipment that needed repair or calibration.

After we had been there for about a year, I got checked out in the T-33 and flew that airplane until we left Japan. It was a single engine jet training plane and great to fly. It was not my first jet airplane, but it was the first one that I was checked out it as 1st pilot.

We finally got to move into base quarters. We sold our "Paddy House" to another military family. We were able to get back the $5,000 that we had paid for the house, but the improvements that we had made were just to make it more comfortable for us while we lived in it. We enjoyed our time in the paddies, but we were glad to move onto the base into better quarters. We did not have a room for our live-in maid, but we had a maid who came every day.

By then we had two little cars with right hand drive and it was easier to drive them than the Thunderbird that we had brought with us when we came over. I had sold the Thunderbird to a Japanese movie producer for about what I had paid for it in Colorado Springs three years before.

As our time in Japan came close to our rotation time, I received the good news that I was promoted to Lt. Colonel. I had a big promotion party at the officers' club and the Japanese really did a super job of decoration for the party. There were two ice sculptures of the oak leave insignia of a Lt. Colonel and they had lights inside of them so that they actually looked silver. The party was a great success. Shortly after my promotion, my boss, the Commander of the Field Maintenance Squadron, rotated to the States and I became the Commander of the Squadron. I served in that position until we rotated back to the States.

Just a couple of months before we were due to rotate; the Chief of Maintenance invited us to his house for dinner. They had a black miniature Poodle and had used him as a stud for a beautiful female Poodle owned by a Japanese person. They had gotten the choice of the litter as stud fee, so they had this cute little black Poodle pup. At one time during the evening, we were sitting on the floor (not uncommon in Japan) and the puppy came over and curled up in Tina's lap. The owner wanted to sell the puppy and he made the smartest suggestion anybody could make. He said, "Why don't you take him home and just see if the kids like him." He knew that there would be no chance that he would ever get that puppy back. We took him home and the next day I paid him for the pup. Our maid was the one who house-broke our new puppy. She would take him outside every hour and stay right with him until he performed.

I received orders for transfer back to the States and my assignment was to Nellis AFB, just outside of Las Vegas, Nevada. We thought that was a pretty good assignment and it was not too far from where my parents lived in California. Soooooooo, off we went. I had arranged for a week's delay in Hawaii on our way home. I had reserved a condo right on Waikiki Beach. The family had a great time during our stay there.

The new puppy, now about 5 months old, flew back to the States on a commercial aircraft and we had some friends pick him up at the airport and take care of him until we got back to the States. We flew back on military aircraft, so the dog had better accommodations than we did. Our tour in Japan was three years and we enjoyed every bit of it. We were all looking forward to our assignment in Las Vegas.

We took a few weeks leave when we got back to the States to see all of the relatives and get used to driving on the right side of the road again. We bought a big Oldsmobile in Madera and I promptly got a ticket for peeling rubber. I was used to those little Japanese cars with no horses under the hood and I just pressed down too hard on the gas pedal on that big Olds. I tried to talk my way out of it, but the judge insisted that I pay my fine, even though he was an old friend from our Madera days.

Chapter 22
Nellis AFB, Las Vegas

I checked into the base, Nellis AFB, at Las Vegas and my assignment was Chief of Maintenance of the Wing. The Wing was a training wing with F-105 aircraft. Our job was to train pilots in the F-105 before they went into combat in Viet Nam. The job of Chief of Maintenance called for a Colonel and here I was, just a brand new Lt. Colonel. I stepped right in and tried to run the job as if I knew what I was doing. I really had a lot of experience in all of the positions below the Chief of Maintenance, so it was not an impossible job. I had also been part of a team, while in Japan, selected to go to Hawaii and write the operating manual for the maintenance operations in Viet Nam. I was familiar with all of the duties of the position of Chief of Maintenance so I made it look as if I had been doing that job my entire career.

It took a few weeks for us to get quarters on the base, so we stayed in a motel that had small apartment units. Even those were kind of a luxury compared to some of our experiences in Japan. There was a pool, so the family had some things to do while I was at work. When we finally got into our quarters they were ½ of a duplex, not on the main part of the base, but an annex. We had to cross a highway to get onto the main part of the base.

After we had been there a short time it became obvious that we needed a second car, so I shopped around and found a used Nash. It looked pretty good and ran alright, but that car really used the oil. I started buying cheap oil and buying it a case at a time. I think that it used about as much oil as it did gas. I also found that Tina was peeling rubber on the rear tires of that big Olds every time that she had to cross the highway to do something on the base. She didn't get caught by the cops like I did, but the kids told on her.

During my time at Nellis, I met and served with some fine people. The commander of the Wing was Colonel Blesse (known as "Boots"). He had served as the Commander of the 366th Fighter Wing in Da Nang, Viet Nam. I was later to become intimately acquainted with that Wing. Boots was the author of a couple of books, "No Guts, No Glory" and "Check Six". He was an ace in the Korean War, shooting down nine MIG's. He was a great Commander and a wonderful person. He later retired as a Major General.

A Colonel was assigned as Deputy for Materiel. He was my boss. His name was Vernon Elarth, but he was known as Tiny. He was anything but tiny. He was about 6 feet, 6 inches tall and weighed about 220 pounds. His hands were like two hams. He was a great guy and very sincere about his job. We got along fine.

We phased out the F-105 training as the F-111's began to arrive. The F-111 was a swing-wing all purpose airplane. The wings swept back when high speed was required. It was McNamara's dream plane. It was supposed to all things, bomber, fighter and carrier capable. We were the first organization to receive the aircraft, as we were to be the training base to train F-111 crews. It was a sturdy aircraft, built with heavy structure in the landing gear to withstand carrier landings. As it turned out, the Navy never took delivery of any of them. It had some great capabilities, but it was very difficult to maintain. It could fly at tree-top level at supersonic speeds. It had terrain-avoidance radar, which would look ahead and cause the airplane to rise over any obstacle in its path. That was a good idea for action against an enemy, as the aircraft could sneak into enemy territory under the radar and toss bombs onto a target and be gone, theoretically, before anyone knew it was there.

The Australians were purchasing F-111's also, so we had Australian ground crew members and flight crew members to train as well as our own personnel.

Shortly after we got our first few F-111's we received word that a new Colonel was arriving into our wing. He was my old boss from Japan, Mac McCarthy. He outranked Tiny, so he was going to be the DM (Director of Materiel). Tiny certainly outranked me, he was a Colonel and I was a Lt. Colonel. So Tiny took my job as Chief of Maintenance. He was really worried about his new boss, McCarthy, and he kept pumping me to learn all he could about him. When Mac arrived, it was like old home week, we had some great get-togethers.

I was moved over to the Field Maintenance Squadron as Squadron Commander. The squadron had about 1450 personnel, so it was a big job, but I was familiar with everything about the squadron. I had been in this position before. During the training of the Australians, I was assigned two Australian exchange officers. They were equivalent in our ranks to a major and a captain. They filled authorized slots in my squadron and served just as an American officer would have served in that position. We became quite close friends during their stay in the US. Those guys were born with hollow legs. They could drink more beer than anyone I had ever seen. Our beer was lower in alcoholic content than the Australian beer was and they could put it down like it was water. I never got over my amazement at their ability to put away the beer.

Shortly after they arrived, I was taking them downtown into the auto sales area. They both wanted to buy a car. (One of them bought a Mustang and took it home with him. He had to buy a kit to convert it to a right hand drive. Australia did not permit cars with the steering on the left.) On the way downtown a roadrunner ran across the road in front of my car. I pointed him out to the two Australians and they were astounded at his size. The only concept that they had of a roadrunner was the cartoon and, in the cartoon, the roadrunner was nearly as big as the coyote. They had been looking for one, but they expected a large bird like the emus of Australia. They were quite disappointed in our scrawny little roadrunner.

The F-111's gave us fits. They were extremely difficult to maintain and our personnel were all learning the intricacies of the various systems of the aircraft. We eventually sent a squadron of

F-111's into Viet Nam and suffered a couple of losses pretty quickly. An old friend of mine from Japan commanded the squadron. The airplane did a pretty good job in combat, but we were not really ready for that job so quickly. McNamara insisted that they go into combat. The aircraft was his idea of a perfect combat aircraft.

Our son, Rick, graduated from High School in Las Vegas. After graduation he was undecided as to what he wanted to do. I told him that I would provide him with a method of going to college, but that he had to work at it. I would pay his tuition and various fees and I would provide him with a certain amount of dollars for each semester hour that he carried with a grade level of C or above. I told him that I didn't intend to be working my fanny off to let him go play around. It was to be a working arrangement for both of us. He mulled that over for a while and then said that he decided that he wanted to join the Navy instead of going to college. A few days later he told me that he had checked with the Navy recruiter in Las Vegas and that there were no openings. I got on the phone to the Naval recruiting office in Los Angeles and they said that they had plenty of openings. Rick was OK with that, but later accused me of shanghaiing him into the Navy. I drove him down to LA and I swore him in. The Navy thought that was great, a Lt. Colonel in the Air Force swearing his son into the Navy. They took pictures of the event.

We had been at Nellis for about three and a half years when I was told that I would be going to Viet Nam as a pilot on a C-47 gunship. There was a big "back to the cockpit" move on in the Air Force. All the guys like me who had been performing duties other than pilot as our principal duty were to be cycled back to the cockpit. That was OK with me; I was a member of the Regular Air Force, not a Reservist on active duty. I always did what I was told to do, but ---- back to a gooney bird. That was kind of an insult. I called the officer in personnel who was responsible for my assignment and suggested that he reconsider my assignment. I told him that I had more than a thousand hours in the RC-121 and also was a qualified maintenance officer on those aircraft and that it might be more appropriate if I shipped out as a pilot on those aircraft rather than the C-47. After due consideration, he agreed and my assignment was changed to the unit that was operating the RC-121's in Viet Nam. Those aircraft were flying radar stations that looked for enemy planes and vectored our fighters into contact with them. They were the same aircraft that I had flown while I was at Otis AFB in Massachusetts. I was due for an overseas assignment and I had no argument with the fact that I was going to Viet Nam.

Since I was going to be flying over Viet Nam, I had to go through the Survival School in the state of Washington. In that school we were taught how to evade the enemy and how to survive if the enemy captured us. I went to Washington and, as it turned out, I was the senior officer in the group going through the training. During the time we were in the simulated Vietnamese prison, the guards always picked on me because I was the senior officer. That is what would happen to me if I were to be captured, so the simulation was realistic. It was a rigorous course that we were put through to prepare us for flying in that area.

When I got back to Nellis there were many other things that had to be done to get ready for my departure. Tina and I decided that it would be better for her and Beckie to live in Madera California while I was gone. My parents were living there and Tina and I had lived there between wars (1946 to 1951), so Tina knew a lot of people there. Rick, our son, was in the Navy. Beckie was finishing her Junior year in High School and we knew that that would be a difficult adaptation for her to go into a new school as a Senior. She knew no one in Madera except her grandparents. I bought a new car so that Tina and Beckie would not have any car trouble while I was gone.

I took a few days off and we went over to Madera and did some house hunting. We found a nice three-bedroom house with a swimming pool. I thought that it would be nice for Beckie to be able to have a pool while I was gone so she could have some kids over for swimming and help her make friends in her new school. Our children made friends easily. They had to, with all the moving that we did. They also adapted easily to new environments.

We moved out of base quarters and into the new house in Madera. I didn't want Tina to have to face that after I was gone. I stayed on the base in bachelor quarters after the move. Our second car was a 1967 Mustang and I sold it to a fellow officer with the provision that I could keep it until I departed Nellis. It was a few weeks until my pending shipment overseas.

The Wing Personnel officer was a good buddy of mine; we played golf together quite a bit. He called me and asked when I was going to leave the base. I had prepared to take three weeks leave at our new home to get things settled before I took off for my year in Viet Nam, so I told him what my planned departure date was. He said that I was not to leave the base on the date that I wanted to leave and that I must stay on the base until a date about five days after I had scheduled my departure. I asked him why I had to stay until that date and he said he could not tell me, but that it was important that I stay until that date. All of this took place in 1970; we had been at Nellis for four years.

I had a suspicion as to the reason that he wanted me to stay those few more days, but I was not sure. I was eligible for promotion to Colonel and I knew that the promotion list was due to be released from the headquarters at about the time that he told me that I must still be on the base. The step-up to Colonel was a really big one and I knew that the chances that I was on the list were very remote. I called Tina in Madera and told her to get reservations and fly over to Las Vegas. She wanted to know why I wanted her to be there and I was very vague about my reasons because I was just guessing and hoping that I was going to be on the promotion list. I didn't want to tell her what I was hoping and then have her be disappointed if my guess was wrong. She came over and I picked her up at the airport. It was great to see her even though we had only been separated for a couple of weeks. I had reserved a room in the guest house at Nellis for us to stay. She was still wondering what had prompted me to have her fly over to Las Vegas.

The day that the personnel officer had told me that I must still be on the base finally arrived and WOW, I was right, I was on the list for promotion to full Colonel. It was a really great happening in my life. That promotion was a huge step. The personnel officer told me that I was on the list and in the same breath he said, "Your assignment to Viet Nam is cancelled. You are now under control of the Colonels' assignment section of Headquarters USAF and they will handle your new assignment. Give them a call at this number."

I called the Colonels' assignment section in the Pentagon and the officer who was in charge of my assignment got on the phone and asked me where I wanted to go. I told him that I had been preparing to go to Viet Nam and that I might as well go there. I was due for a tour there and, since I had bought a house, a new car and moved the family, I might just as well go and get it over with. I think that it kind of shocked him for someone to say "Send me to Viet Nam". He said he would call me back after he got my assignment straightened out.

In the meantime, Tina and I were arranging with the Officers Club to have a promotion party before we departed. Lots of things were going on. Tina got busy with the club on the party and I was scurrying around the clearing the base and getting ready for final departure from Nellis. It was a wonderful and hectic time. It all came together. I was given my new assignment, which was as Chief of Maintenance of a fighter wing at Phan Rang in Viet Nam, and the party at the Officers Club was all arranged.

The party at Nellis was a huge success. I was the only officer in the Wing who had made the promotion list to Colonel. We had lots of friends there and they all were all pleased about my promotion. Tina had been very active in the Officers' Wives Club while we were at Nellis. She had managed a thrift shop that the Wives Club operated on the base and was well known and well liked. It was a grand time and a wonderful way to say our "Good-byes" again. We flew over to Madera and a whole new chapter in our life started.

Chapter 23
Viet Nam --- Phan Rang & Da Nang

Our house in Madera was a nice one in a relatively new neighborhood. There were several things that I wanted to do to make the house more comfortable for Tina and Beckie while I was gone. I moved the washer and dryer connections from a pantry, off of the kitchen, to the garage and built a lot of shelves in the pantry. There was a large covered patio, which was fairly close to the pool. I carpeted the patio floor so there would be a nice area for lounging. We did a lot of painting and touching up. I wanted Tina and Beckie to be comfortable and cozy while I was gone for a year.

The front door of the house was a big double door and Tina decided that it should be painted Chinese Red, so Beckie was given the job of painting the doors. I told Beckie that it would require two coats of the red paint to make it look nice. We sanded the door in preparation for the painting and I went on to another job. I came back out front in a short time and the door was painted and the paint was all bubbled and puckered. Beckie had given the doors their two coats, but had not waited for the first one to dry before applying the second coat. She had never painted anything like that before and did not know that the first coat had to be dry before applying the second coat. We all got a big kick out of that. Of course, we had to sand it down again and then we finally got it painted. Those bright red doors really lit up the neighborhood.

I finally got all packed and flew commercial to Seattle and from there, departed for Viet Nam via chartered flight. We flew to Anchorage on the first leg of the flight and then to Yokota Air Base in Japan. It was late afternoon when we departed Anchorage and the sun was fairly low in the sky. As we flew west the sun stayed about the same in the sky. We were chasing the sun and going fast enough at those northern latitudes that we just about kept up with the world spinning. I thought that was interesting to see the sun stay almost in the same spot for hours. As our great circle route took us farther to the south, the sun finally got to set.

We had some time in Yokota for flight crew change and servicing the aircraft. While we were waiting there, I got in touch with Ed Cannon, who had been the navigator on the B-17 crew that I went to England with. He had stayed in the service and was also a full Colonel and was the Base Civil Engineer at Yokota AFB. We chatted for quite a bit. I had not seen Ed since way back at Castle AFB when I was doing my Reserve duty there, before I was recalled.

Our flight resumed and we finally arrived in Viet Nam. We landed at the air base at Cam Ran Bay. It was hot and humid, very much so. It was late at night and my time world was so upset that my body had no idea whether it was night or day. We were about half way around the world from where I had started. My poor old body just knew that it was very tired and needed sleep. I checked in to the Officers' Billeting and was given a room in a "hooch". (My new rank was not effective yet, so I was not being given the treatment that a full Colonel would get. The date that my promotion was to be effective was the 1st of January 1971. I still had several months as a Lt. Colonel before the big day when I got to pin on those eagles.) The hooch had air conditioning and that was a blessing. I slept hard for several hours and then got up when it was still dark and tried to get something to eat. The mess hall was open and I was really hungry, so I had a big breakfast and then started trying to arrange transportation to Phan Rang.

There was a big air terminal there with military flights going to all parts of South Viet Nam. I got on the list for Phan Rang and just had to wait until there was a plane going there. It was late in the afternoon before I got out of Cam Ran Bay on my way to Phan Rang. I arrived at Phan Rang at about six in the evening. I got out of the plane and, with all of my luggage, made my way into the base operations office. I got a base phone book and looked up the Deputy Commander for Materiel (DM), my new boss. I expected to be welcomed with opened arms, here I was, just on the list for promotion to full Colonel and assigned by the colonels' assignment section from the Pentagon as the Chief of Maintenance of the 35th Tactical Fighter Wing. I called the Colonel who was the Wing DM. When he answered the phone I said, "This is Colonel Bushong and I am down at base ops. He said, "Who are you?" I said, "I am your new Chief of Maintenance." I had supposed that the Pentagon would have advised him that I was coming and that he would know who I was. He said, "I already have a Chief of Maintenance." That really set me back on my heels. I knew that someone was doing that job while I was on my way there, but his statement was so abrupt and final that I really felt like crawling under the desk. He said, "Oh all right, I'll be down to get you in a few minutes." but that was said without any enthusiasm. What a great welcoming.

He took me up to the billeting office and left me there. He said he would see me tomorrow and we would get everything straightened out. I was completely pooped and disgusted by this time. I was assigned a room and made my way there and dropped off my bags and went over to the Officer's Club to get something to eat. The officers' mess was closed; wouldn't you know it. I finally got a sandwich at a snack bar and then went to my room and went to bed.

Phan Rang was a busy place. All night long there was artillery fire going on. I didn't know who they were shooting at, but they sure were making a lot of noise. I went to sleep quickly and slept fitfully until about 2:30 AM. My body was not adjusted to the time difference and I guess that it was time to get up in some part of the world. I knew that it took about a day for each hour of time change to get properly adjusted and I had had about a 12-hour change from when I left California. I got up and got dressed and went outside to see my new world. I stood there in the dark, leaning on a wall and watched airplanes taking off and could see the artillery fire near the base. At that time I was not feeling very chipper. I think that was one of the lowest points in my entire military career. Here I was, my time was all screwed up, I was not wanted in the job that I had been assigned and I was standing in a strange land watching a war in the middle of the night. I had always adapted easily to new environments and conditions, but I was not comfortable about this situation.

I walked over to the officer's mess and had breakfast. That made me feel a little better. At a decent hour, around 7 AM, I made my way to the office of the DM. He told me to go down to the maintenance complex and meet the Chief of Maintenance and stay with him while he contacted the Pentagon to get it straightened out. He also told me that his Chief of Maintenance was on the promotion list to Colonel and would assume the new rank in a few weeks. It turned out that he was on the tail end of the previous year's Colonel's list and that was possibly the reason that the personnel officer did not catch his error when he sent me there. There was a Lt. Colonel in the job and the job called for a full Colonel. He, however, was going to be a Colonel before I was. My effective date was the 1st of January 1971 and his was a day in September of 1970. I could see why the DM said that he had a Chief of Maintenance and he sure didn't need me.

The DM got on the phone to the Colonel's assignment section in Washington and they were very apologetic and said that they would get it straightened out quickly. In the meantime, I was busy in the maintenance complex seeing how the operation went. The wing was equipped with F-100's and there was also a wing of Vietnamese aircraft on the base. The Vietnamese were flying A-37 airplanes, advanced jet trainers that had been converted to combat airplanes. We used to call them "teeny-weeny noisemakers", but the Vietnamese were using them as dive-bombers and doing a pretty good job with them.

It was interesting to me to see how the maintenance operation proceeded, since I had been on a team in Hawaii who were tasked to write the maintenance operating procedures for the South East Asia operations. This had happened while I was stationed in Japan and the Viet Nam operation was just being built up. I was now going to have to operate under rules that I had been instrumental in writing. The maintenance operation of the

Phan Rang wing seemed to be going very well. It was good for me to get to wander around and check into the many areas of responsibility of the Chief of Maintenance.

It was a few days before the Colonel's assignment section in Washington got me a new assignment and faxed a new set of orders to me. In the meantime, I was learning a lot about the maintenance operation of a Fighter Wing in Southeast Asia. Every evening we would have dinner at the Officer's Club and after dinner we would go out on the patio and watch the war. The Club was on top of a hill and from the patio we could see artillery fire and dive-bombers dropping their bombs on the Viet Cong. I was amazed that the bad guys were that close to the base. It was quite a show and was performed day and night when the weather permitted. It was more visible at night with all the flashes of the exploding bombs and artillery shells. My body's time clock had finally almost reset itself to Vietnamese time and I could sleep at night and stay awake in the daytime.

My new assignment was to the 366th Tactical Fighter Wing at Da Nang AFB. Da Nang was the northernmost airbase in South Viet Nam. It was the closest one to the DMZ (demilitarized zone). I took a little ribbing before I left Phan Rang about going from the frying pan into the fire. Da Nang was called "Rocket Alley" because the North Vietnamese fired Russian made rockets into the base so frequently. At that time, I really didn't care. I just wanted to get situated into a job and get to work.

There was no regularly scheduled flight from Pan Rang to Da Nang, so I had to catch a ride back to Cam Ran Bay and then wait for a flight to Da Nang. That took another full day. I was pooped when I got to Da Nang, but my reception there was quite different. I was met at the aircraft and escorted to the DV (distinguished visitor) quarters where I had a room for the night.

That first night at Da Nang, about 1:00 AM, there was an announcement on the "Giant Voice" which was a bunch of huge speakers all over the base. The nearest one to where I was staying was right over the top of the building and that voice was really GIANT. The announcement was, "DA NANG IS UNDER

ATTACK -- DA NANG IS UNDER ATTACK -- TAKE COVER -- TAKE COVER" There was a small carpet on the concrete floor next to my bunk. I rolled out of bed onto that carpet and listened for the rockets to go off. I heard several explosions, none close to me, and then the "All Clear" came over the Giant Voice. I crawled back into bed and slept soundly the rest of the night.

The next day I was to move into my permanent quarters which were a two-bedroom mobile home to be shared with another Colonel who was the Assistant Deputy for Operations of the wing. It turned out that he was an old friend of mine from previous bases. We had first met in Japan and then again at Nellis AFB in Nevada.

The quarters for all the Colonels in the Wing were on both sides of a short street leading to the Officer's Club. They were all mobile homes and were shared except for the Wing Commander who had a mobile home all to himself. The quarters that I was to occupy was presently being used by the Lt. Colonel who had been serving in the position of Chief of Maintenance. That was the job that I was taking and the quarters went with the job, so he had to move. He was doing the job that called for a Colonel while they waited for a full Colonel to arrive. I don't know why the Colonel's assignment section didn't catch that in the first place. Frank Kerchner was the Lt. Colonel who had been doing that job and now he had to move down and I was to take the job, the quarters and his jeep. It was quite a letdown for him. He actually outranked me as a Lt. Colonel. His date of rank was before mine, but he had not made the promotion list to full Colonel and I had, so I got the job, jeep and quarters. Frank had to move out of the mobile home into a hooch, which was smaller quarters, and without the luxury of a kitchen and refrigerator. Frank had been there for a while and had a stock of whiskey so I bought his share of the booze.

The transition to quarters and job took place over the next couple of days. Frank became the Maintenance Control Officer and I moved into the Chief of Maintenance job. It was not a new responsibility for me. I had been Chief of Maintenance of a wing before, but I had to learn my way around the base and the aircraft were new to me.

We were equipped with the F-4 (Phantom) aircraft. They were a very powerful twin-engine fighter, capable of speeds of more than Mach 2 (twice the speed of sound). The primary use was for dive-bombing with high explosive bombs and with napalm bombs. They were also an effective fighter for engaging the Russian MIG's that the North Vietnamese were using. In addition to the bombs, they carried heat seeking missiles and radar guided missiles. The later models had a built in Gattling gun which fired 20 MM projectiles at a rate of 6,000 rounds per minute. There had been an adaptation on the earlier models of the F-4 so that a Gattling gun in a pod could be hung under the airplane on the center-line and used in a dogfight with the MIG's. The Wing had gotten the nickname of "The Gunfighters" because of their ability to carry and fight with the 20 MM gun hanging under the aircraft. "Boots" Blesse had been the Wing Commander when they first got the gun and I am sure that he had a lot to do with the nickname.

During my processing into the wing I had a nice meeting with the Wing Commander and he welcomed me to the organization. During our conversation he mentioned that my job as Chief of Maintenance did not call for flying and therefore I was excused from flying. That meant that I did not get to fly but would receive my flight pay during the time that I was there. I said, "I am going to be here for a year and I really would like to fly the F-4." He groaned and said that he would try to get special permission for me to fly.

He got the permission in a few days and then I was required to go back to the Philippines to go through the "Jungle Survival School". I had only been there a couple of weeks and then went back to the Philippines for a week. To fly in South East Asia it was required that one complete the jungle survival course. It was known as "Snake School" because of the snakes that were around the jungle where we had to survive for a few days after we had completed the ground school portion. We were taught to get food and water from the jungle plants so that we could survive until we might get picked up by the rescue helicopters (Jolly Green Giants). We were also taught how to hide in the jungle to perhaps evade the enemy.

During our hiding phase we were given two wooden plaques. We were to do our best to hide and then a group of native children were sent out to try to find us. If we were found, we were to give one of the plaques to the kid who found us and it was good for a pound of rice. We were easy picking for those kids. They found all of us twice except one guy who climbed to the top of a palm tree and hid in the fronds. He was not found and had a hell of a time getting down when the search was over.

During our stay in the jungle we had a Negrito (small native of the Philippines) guide. He showed us the places where we could get food and water in the jungle and how to prepare the food. He also showed us how to make a bed and sleep on the jungle floor. WOW, that jungle is really a noisy place at night. There are all sorts of creepy-crawly things moving around. A lot of the jungle animals are nocturnal and did their thing while we were trying to sleep there amongst them. I was lucky; I was the senior officer in the group, so the Negrito guide made my bed out of banana leaves to demonstrate to the other members of the survival group. There were 10 of us plus the Negrito and a GI guide.

We also got to practice being snatched out of the jungle by helicopter. We had to guide the helicopter to our position using the emergency radio and then we were snatched out of the jungle on a cable *What fun.* (Remember, I was 47 years old at that time, no longer a spring chicken, and what was fun for some of the younger guys was, sometimes, not so much fun for me.)

By the time I finished that survival school I was ready to survive any situation in the whole world. I had completed the Artic Survival School, Sea Survival School, Prisoner of War Survival School and Jungle Survival School. All I had to do was get back to Viet Nam and start surviving. I flew back to Da Nang in a noisy C-130 and dug into my job. I did not tell Tina that I was going to be flying while I was in Viet Nam. She had enough on her hands running the house back in California without worrying about me flying. She knew that I was the Chief of Maintenance and that my job did not call for flying. Our son, Rick, was in the Navy and I told him that I was flying, but told him not to tell his Mom.

My job was a seven-day a week job. I usually got up about 0430 and had breakfast and then went to my maintenance control room and got myself up-to-date on the condition of each airplane that was not in commission. I had to know what needed to be done to bring them into commission and what parts were needed to do that. Every day but Sunday we had a command briefing at 0700, so I had to get all the information for that meeting. I usually had one of my officers from the maintenance control center do the detailed briefing, but I also wanted to know everything that he was going to brief the staff about. My day continued until about 7 or 8 that evening. My Sunday was a little different. We did not have a staff briefing at 0700. I usually got up a little later, around 0600 and I wore different clothes on Sunday. I wore a tan uniform shirt and trousers instead of the jungle fatigues that I wore every other day. I also took an hour off to go to church each Sunday. That made it an entirely different day for me. I did about the same things during the rest of the day. The time passed fairly quickly for me since I was always busy and it was soon approaching the date that I would pin on the eagles of a full Colonel.

When I had arrived at Da Nang I had been issued three sets of two-piece jungle fatigues. I took them to the tailor shop and had the sleeves cut off and name tags, wings and rank insignia sewn on each set. As the time approached to wear the new rank, I took a set over and had the eagles sewn on. The rank insignias that we wore over there on our flight suits and fatigues were dark in color, not shiny or white. That was so that the bad guys could not see them as easily and pick off the officers. (Good thinking).

Behind the maintenance control building, the GI's had built a lean-to. They had acquired a freezer from somewhere and had it stocked with a variety of fish and steaks. They had made a barbeque from an old steel drum and they had some of their social functions back there. They had built some tables and benches and it was kind of a neat place. I had been invited there for a steak a few times and it was quite nice.

We had one Master Sergeant who was a super scrounger. Every outfit had to have a guy like that. He could start out at mid-day with a couple of sheets of plywood and a gallon of paint, or something like that, and come back in the evening with a case of New York cut steaks. We had a wing of Marines on the base, a wing of Vietnamese fighters, the Jolly Green Giants and a squadron of gun-ships. There were lots of places where a good scrounger could exercise his talents. The larder in the lean-to was kept stocked by his efforts.

I decided to have my promotion party in the lean-to on New Years Eve. My promotion was effective the next day and I thought it appropriate that I give a party for the key NCO's and the officers of the maintenance complex who worked so hard to make me look like I knew what I was doing. There were about 1450 people in the maintenance complex. We could not have them all, but a few of the ones I worked with on a daily basis. So it was all arranged. I bought all the booze and beer and the scrounger furnished the steaks and other food. It was a grand party and just before midnight the Wing Commander appeared. He joined in the party and everyone had a grand time. He had a huge set of eagles, about a foot long, that he pinned on me at midnight. All the guys got a big kick out of that.

A couple of days later, at the morning briefing, the base Civil Engineer said that he had never seen so smooth a transition from Lt. Colonel to Colonel as the one I made. He said, "It was amazing, one day your were a Lt. Colonel and the next you were a full Colonel with no fuss or anything. The insignia changed on your collar, but you were the same and doing the same job." I thanked him for the complement. I just felt that was the way it should work. I had been in full Colonel's positions since just after I was promoted to Lt. Colonel. I don't want to pretend that being promoted to Colonel wasn't a big thing in my life; it was.

It was about that time when a new Dodge pickup arrived and was assigned to me as a replacement for my Jeep. It was a welcome change for me. The Dodge was a lot better riding than the Jeep. The first thing that I did was to send it over to the paint shop and have them paint the top of the cab white. I spent a lot of hours in the hot sun in my vehicle and I figured that the white top might lower the temperature in the cab a few degrees. The pickup was radio equipped, as had been my Jeep, so I could stay in contact with Maintenance Control no matter where I was in the base. Of course, my call sign was "Maintenance One".

Just after I got my new wheels and the new paint job, I passed the Wing Commander in his staff car. He saw my new pickup with the white top and just about blew his top. He got hold of me by phone when I was back in my office and said, "What are you doing, painting the top of a GI vehicle white? You are not supposed to do that. They are all supposed to be Air Force blue." I explained the benefit to me of the couple of degrees cooler during the hours that I spent out in the extensive maintenance area and then I thought of another benefit. I said, "And think of this, Colonel, you can spot me anyplace on the base and you will immediately know it is me because of the white top. If we ever want it back to blue, it will only take my Field Maintenance paint shop a few minute to get it done." He said, "OK, I'll let you get by with it."

The white top on the pickup had another advantage. As I was prowling around throughout the maintenance complex, all of the maintenance personnel knew I was there observing them.

The rocket attacks by the Viet Cong occurred a couple of times a week, usually at night, and usually six to eight rockets during each attack. One night our bomb dump was hit. The bomb dump was where all of the bombs were stored and prepared for use before being brought to the aircraft. The bomb dump was very large and was broken into small areas with berms of earth around each one to contain potential explosions and keep the whole bomb dump from being demolished. I went out to the dump to see what the damage was and was astounded to see that the rocket had hit under a pallet of 500 lb. bombs and the explosion of the rocket had tossed the bombs all around the revetment. None of them had exploded, which was fortunate; but they were not fused and not supposed to explode until they were fused. The explosion could have detonated one and then we could have had a chain reaction and others exploded. The bomb dump had been hit several years before and had a massive chain reaction. I had seen movies of that episode.

After I had finished in the bomb dump area, I noticed that the paved road went onward past the bomb dump area, so I decided to continue on down the road to see what was out there. The road was in pretty good shape and I drove out for about six or eight miles. I was driving along with the windows open and all of a sudden, I heard small arms (rifle) fire. I stopped and looked around and spotted some troops (Vietnamese) out to my left about a half-mile away. They were shooting, then getting up and running forward and flopping down and shooting again. I can tell you that my pickup made the fastest U turn in history and peeled rubber heading back to the base. I really did not want any more bullet holes in any machine while I was in it, be it airplane or pickup.

Chapter 24
Da Nang, Viet Nam

As I mentioned, my quarters were on the street leading to the Officers Club. The street was only about a block long and had concrete sidewalks along both sides of the street. One night, the Jolly Green Giants (rescue helicopter squadron) painted huge green footprints on the sidewalk in front of my quarters all the way to the Club. They were about three feet long. Everybody got a big kick out of the footprints. About three nights later, the Medics painted a big band-aid on the big toe of every foot. Each band-aid had a red cross painted on the pad. That got another laugh out of everybody.

One of the areas of my responsibility was the munitions squadron and all of their activities, guns, bombs, bomb racks, loading of munitions and storage of munitions. Before I arrived at Da Nang, someone had put a 500 lb. bomb in my front yard. It was about ½ buried in the ground. I guess they thought it was appropriate that the Chief of Maintenance have his quarters marked with a part of the Munitions Squadron. One day, I was coming out of my quarters after lunch and some guys were walking down the sidewalk toward the club. I heard one of them say, "My God, look at that. That bomb landed here and didn't go off. Boy, was he lucky." I got a kick out of that and stayed out of sight until they moved on to the club. It was good to get a chuckle once in a while, because things were pretty tense and I worked extremely long hours.

I almost forgot to tell you about my dog. When I moved into the office of the Chief of Maintenance there was a dog there. He was a typical Vietnamese dog, tan, about 35 pounds and his tail curled up over his back. I think all the Vietnamese dogs that I saw had that tail curled up over their back. He came with the job. His home was the Chief of Maintenance's office. He kind of watched me for a few days with his eyes kind of rolled up when I came into the office. I guess he wanted to see if I was going to stay. After a few days he adopted me as his boss. He came with me when I moved around the building from my office into the maintenance control center. He truly became my dog. The guys around the office kept him fed and watered, but he went with the job of the Chief. He often went with me when I traveled around through the maintenance complex. He especially liked it when my jeep was turned in for the new Dodge pickup.

He would run out with me when I had to go somewhere in my pickup and jump into the back of the pickup. He never tried to ride in the cab with me. I always was amused by his antics whenever we stopped and there was another dog in the area. If the other dog was larger than he was, he stayed in the back of the pickup and growled. If the other dog was smaller than he was he would jump down and chase them. He was no dummy. He didn't mess with those dogs that were bigger than he was. He had a few scars around his ears and head when I first met him. I suppose that is how he learned not to tangle with those bigger dogs. The guys had named him "Admin" because he lived in the building called Maintenance Administration.

He stuck pretty close to me whenever I was around and loved to ride in the pickup. My quarters were about three and a half miles from my office and I would often go up there for a snack at lunch time. He rode up with me, but he did not seem to want to go into my quarters. He stayed outside on the front porch and several times he rode the bus back to the office if I didn't leave quickly enough to suit him. That was something. There was a base bus that made the circle from the quarters area down to the offices that were at the extreme distances. The bus made the circuit pretty frequently. Admin knew about the bus and knew that it went from the quarters area back to his home on the flight line. The drivers seemed to know Admin and let him ride the bus. He knew when to get off. If he was not there when I came out of my quarters during the day I knew he would be back in the office when I got there. He never attempted to ride with me at night when I was going home to stay.

About a month or so after I got settled into the routine, my trailer mate got a new alarm clock. That would not be a big deal except what happened to me because of that new clock. One morning I was a little late getting going and I was rushing around to get out of the quarters and get to work. It was about 0530 instead of my usual 0430. To set the stage properly for this story, I have to tell you about our living room. There was a desk and chair on one side of the room where we could write or study. The night before I had been writing letters at the desk and had neglected to push the chair all the way back to the desk when I had finished. As I was scurrying around trying to get dressed and out of there, my trailer mate's new alarm clock went off. I had never heard it before because I was always gone before he got up. It was a buzzing sound --- our doorbell also was a buzzing sound. I thought, "My God, I am so late that they are coming to get me." I thought that someone from my office was buzzing the doorbell on our trailer. I ran from my bedroom toward the front door and, in the dark, hit the chair in front of the desk. I came down on the straight back chair <u>hard.</u> I was straddling the back of the chair. It hurt like hell. I struggled off the chair and went to the front door. Of course, there was no one there.

I finished dressing and went to work. I got my morning briefing quickly and went to the staff briefing. I was still hurting, but could move around OK. Things were busy, as usual, and I spent the rest of the day doing whatever I had to do. I got home about 2030 (8:30 PM), dog tired and not feeling very perky. I peeled off my fatigues and the crotch of the pants was soaked with blood. My shorts were also soaked. I examined myself and found that there was a hole in my scrotum where I had come down on the back of that chair. I had been going all day with that hole, about 3/4 of an inch long. I was so exhausted and felt so bad that I just went to bed and said to myself, "I'll take care of it tomorrow.

The next morning, after staff meeting, I went over to the Flight Surgeon and told him what had happened. He looked at my wound and shook his head. He said, "I can't sew it up now

126

because you have left it open for so long and there is no telling what you have allowed in there. I would just be sewing the germs inside of you. It will just have to heal from the inside out. You must soak in hot water for at least 15 minutes twice a day." I had a tub in my bathroom in the mobile home, so I could comply with his instructions. He dressed the wound and gave me some ointment and sterile pads to dress it myself. At that moment I had the only *air-cooled balls* in Viet Nam and it was not too pleasant.

I had been scheduled to go TDY to Phan Rang for a few days and he made me promise to check in with the Flight Surgeon there. I did and he made arrangements for my hot soaks each day in a big tub in the hospital. A lot of people got a big kick out of my air-cooled balls. The wound finally healed and everything was fine.

Shortly after the first of the year, the DM, my boss, rotated back to the States. I was then the only Colonel in the Materiel Directorate, so I got the job as DM until a new Colonel arrived to take the position. As DM I was in charge of the Maintenance and Supply organizations. Of course, I was familiar with all of the Maintenance functions and, I was acquainted with the Supply functions, but had never been in charge of them. Taking that job meant that I had to move into the DM's office, which was located in the Wing Headquarters building, about a mile from my office. I moved into the DM office and settled into the job. Frank Kerstner moved back into the Chief of Maintenance job. I knew that it was just temporary, until the new DM arrived, so I did not change my mail address. Mail was very important to everyone over there. It was our contact with the real world. My mail was being delivered to the Chief of Maintenance office and then would be brought up to the DM office whenever other correspondence or reports needed to brought up.

There was a small staff in the DM office, one Lieutenant, a couple of NCOs and two Vietnamese clerks. There was an empty desk where there had been one more NCO at a previous time. The holder for the name plate of the occupant was empty, so I thought we would have a little fun. I had one of the NCOs make a name plate for S/Sgt. Mary Louise Gray and put it on the empty desk. Then when one of the guys brought the mail up and saw the name plate, we told him that there was a really good looking WAF assigned to the DM office. Immediately the official correspondence and my mail started to arrive much more frequently. The secret was kept strictly in the DM office. It was a kick to see those GI's come in with such an eager look on their faces. Everyone in the DM office was telling all of them how good looking the WAF Sgt. was, and they were practically drooling. We had to keep thinking up places for her to be when they came into the office. We said that she was able to take dictation and that sometimes the Wing Commander had her come to his office to do that for him. Sometimes she was at the Base Exchange. Occasionally she would have to be at other parts of the base when they came in. Several of the ones in the know kept talking about what a striking girl she was. She was really a beauty. The mail was coming up from the Chief of Maintenance office and other parts of the complex at a rapid rate.

One day, after our fictitious WAF had been there for a few days, I saw a Red Cross Lady in the hallway of the Headquarters. I asked her if she would do us a favor. She was willing, so the favor was to call my old office and say that the caller was S/Sgt Gray and ask if Colonel Bushong had any mail there to be brought up to the DM's office. I let her in on our hoax and asked her to use her most sexy voice. She completed the call and within a few minutes there were a couple of the NCOs from the Maintenance building up there with something in their hands. We had to tell them that she had just left and that they should have seen her in the hallway as they came in. They had not seen her and were very disappointed. After a couple of weeks we transferred the fictitious WAF to Saigon. We made a set of orders for her transfer, and told the guys that it was a mistake for her to be sent there in the first place. There were no WAFs on Da Nang. We had a lot of fun with our imaginary WAF and she did improve the correspondence delivery system.

In the meantime, I had gone through a short ground

school on the ejection seat of the F-4 and was ready to go flying. I think that my first flight was on a test flight, and that was quite appropriate, since I still had the AFSC (Air Force Specialty Code) of Flight Test Officer in my records. I never did get checked out in the front seat of the F-4. That required a special transition school back in the States. Each time I flew in the F-4, I was in the back seat and a qualified F-4 pilot was in the front seat. I did get to handle the aircraft and it was a real thrill for me. It was a great performance aircraft. For example, on the test flights, the aircraft had to perform properly at all speeds up to Mach 2.1 (about 1500 MPH) in addition to other test procedures. I got to fly on several test flights and each one was a kick. I did go on some combat sorties, but the boss was very careful where I went and I always had a well qualified pilot in the front seat. I suppose it was an imposition on the other pilots to take me on a flight, but it was great for me. I was always the GIB (guy in back), but I did get to fly the airplane. The guys that I flew with were always generous with the stick time so I got a lot of time on the controls, made take-offs, landings and instrument approaches. It was a fun airplane to fly.

While I was DM I inspected all areas of supply and one site was a few acres of 55 gallon drums of "Agent Orange" which was a chemical that had been used to defoliate forest areas that the Viet Cong were occupying so that they could be spotted from the air. The chemical had been sprayed from aircraft over large parts of the jungle. It was no longer being used, but we had thousands of gallons in storage. I suppose that a way to dispose of it had not yet been devised. During my inspection of the area where it was stored I got out of my pick-up and strolled through the barrels. Some of them were leaking and I got some of the chemical on my boots. I reported the leaks to the proper authorities. Later it was discovered that exposure to Agent Orange caused cancer, specifically, prostate cancer, and sure enough I was diagnosed with prostate cancer in 1991. Little did I know that wading around in the stuff in 1971 would cause that to happen to me in 1991.

The new DM arrived and I went back to the Chief of Maintenance job. I had put my name on the list for an R&R (rest & relaxation) trip to Australia. My name finally came up and off I went to Sydney for a week. It was good to get out of the rat race at Da Nang and see how the real world looked. I had never been to Australia and it was a real thrill for me. It was good to sleep in every morning and stay out late at night. I enjoyed the city of Sydney and the surrounding area. The people there were very friendly to the US troops who came there for R&R. I guess they realized that they had been through some pretty rough times.

Before I left for Australia, several NCOs asked me if I would pick up some raw opals for them while I was there. There was a lapidary shop on base where they could grind and polish gems. They had the address of a particular shop in Sydney and about six guys gave me specific orders on what exact raw opal stock they wanted and each of them gave me a check. After I got settled into my hotel in Sydney, I took a cab to the opal dealer's shop. I was astounded at all the opals in the shop. Each of the orders that I had was for a certain number of ounces of a certain quality of raw opal stock. The gentleman who ran the shop was very kind and he could see that I knew absolutely nothing about opals so he very carefully weighed and marked each order for each person. After he finished with all of the orders that I had he asked if I was going to buy any for myself. I said, "It is pretty obvious that I know nothing about opals. I would not have any idea of what to buy." He said, "Why don't you let me pick out a couple of ounces of this $15 per ounce stock. I'll pick you out some really good pieces from this box." He did and I thought, "How could I go wrong for $30" so I bought the two ounces. There were about eight pieces of opal stock in those two ounces. The orders that I had for the guys back at Da Nang were much more expensive per ounce. Mine was the cheap stuff.

After my week was up in Sydney, I returned to Da Nang, refreshed and ready to go to work. I delivered the opals to the NCOs and told a couple of them that they owed me a lesson on what to do to opal stock to make an opal. They said, "OK, you come over to the lapidary shop after you finish your day and we'll show you what to do."

I finished work a little early that day, around 1830 (6:30 PM), got a snack and took my $30 bag of opals over to the lapidary shop. There were about 20 guys there grinding away on various types of stones. One of the NCOs that I had purchased opals for was there and took me through the process of turning a raw opal into a gem. He took my bag of opals and shook them out into a tray and picked out one piece. From then on, I did everything, with him telling me what had to be done. By the end of the evening I had a beautiful opal all ground and polished. I said, "Wow, that is beautiful. What is it worth?" He said, "come over to the scales and we'll weigh it. " That opal weighed 11 carats. I asked him what a carat was worth and he said that the quality of the stone that I had in my hand was about $20 per carat. I was overjoyed. Here I had a stone worth about $220 and I had gotten it out of my package of $30 raw opals and had spent about 2 ½ hours grinding and polishing it. It was cut to a standard size, so he asked me if I wanted a mount for it. The guys who did that work on a regular basis had an inventory of mounts that they had bought. I bought a mount for it and made a pendant out of it that very night. I was so proud of it that I became an *Opalholic* right there and then. I was hooked. It was a good way to pass a few hours each evening after a hard and long day of work. I ground a lot of opals and took some of them to Bangkok when I could get there and had a jeweler make them into rings and pendants. All of my relatives received packages with opal rings in them. I even gave one to my Vietnamese maid. The other maids said that she did the laundry with one hand held high out of the water after I gave her that ring.

That reminds me, I must tell you about my maid. My trailer-mate and I paid her a few dollars a week and she cleaned the trailer, did our laundry and polished out boots. Any clothes that we left on the floor were washed. There was a clothes line in the back yard of our trailer, but she would not use it. She insisted on laying the wet clothes on the grass and bushes to dry. It worked out OK except a little grass burr in the clothes occasionally.

Our maid was 38 years old and had 11 children. She was about 25 inches around all the way from her shoulders to her knees. There was not a visible curve on her body. She had shiny, coal-black teeth from chewing beetle nuts all her life. She did not smile very much, but when she did, it was amazing to see those shiny black teeth. I tried for a long time to get a picture of her when she was smiling so I could show her teeth, but I think she was wise to that trick and would not smile when the camera was around.

We had four monsoon seasons there in Southeast Asia. They alternated between a dry monsoon and a wet one with the flow of air coming from opposite directions for each. The dry ones were not very dry. We also had one typhoon while I was there. A typhoon is a hurricane except it is called by a different name in that part of the world. I was out in the typhoon trying to make sure that all of our planes and equipment were secure. We had some small losses, but not bad.

In the spring I was selected as the representative for the Far Eastern Air Force to be a member of a promotion board at the Air Force Personnel Office in San Antonio, Texas. The board was to select the Majors who were to be promoted to Lt. Colonel the next year. I was excited about the trip. I came back to the States on a chartered aircraft and stopped in California. I got Tina and we flew into San Antonio on commercial aircraft and got quarters at Randolph Field where the promotion board was to be held. What a deal!!! Here I was in the middle of a tour in Viet Nam and I was ensconced with my wife in VIP quarters in Randolph Field, the old home of the Air Force. The board was scheduled to take two weeks to make the required number of selections. The board consisted of Colonels and Generals. All Majors who were eligible for promotion were considered, but the number to be selected was limited by the number of vacancies.

The process was quite orderly. The board was broken into panels with one General and four colonels on each panel. We read the history and ratings of each candidate and assigned a grade to each one. If there were a large disparity between ratings by various individuals, that record would be discussed and resolved by the panel before sending our recommendation forward. It was a tedious and demanding procedure and extremely important to the people that we were considering. I found the board very interesting.

Tina and I had some nice evenings together, dinner and strolls along the famous river in San Antonio. The board did not meet for the weekend so I suggested to Tina that I rent an airplane and we fly up to Kansas and get her sister and husband and then all of us fly up to Nebraska and see Tina's brother and his wife. She agreed, so we went out to a local airfield and I negotiated four place aircraft for the weekend. The owner asked me if I had a pilot's license and I told him that I did, but it was over in Viet Nam (it really was over there). He said, "Well, I'll just let you fly me around the pattern a couple of times and make a couple of landings and I'll know if you can fly OK." We did that and he was satisfied that I knew how to fly so off we went.

Tina's sister and brother-in-law had never been in a small plane before so it was a real kick for them. I had Joe in the copilot's seat and, after we got underway, I let him fly it. We had a great visit and returned everybody to home and Tina and I went back to San Antonio.

The promotion board lasted for another week. During our work on the promotion board, we had to review each eligible officer's records and the OERs (Officer Effectiveness Report) were of special interest to us because they were a verbal description of how the officer performed his duties and took on other responsibilities. The OER was written by the officer's immediate supervisor, then endorsed by the officer at the next level, and occasionally endorsed by the third level of supervision. The comments by the originating officer were several paragraphs and each succeeding endorsement was generally shorter. There were two endorsements made by General Officers that I will never forget. One was, "If initiative were a snowflake, this officer would be a veritable blizzard." the other was, "This officer is the type who will go through life pushing on doors plainly marked PULL." Each of those two comments told a lot about the officer in a very few words -- they were classic. They were read aloud to the entire board.

When our selection process finished each of the officers who served went our separate ways. I, of course went back to Viet Nam. Boy, it was tough to drop Tina in Madera, see my folks for a day, and then back to Da Nang.

I got back to Da Nang and into the rat-race again. There was a constant rotation of personnel in the maintenance complex, so it was a continual training job for supervisors and supervisors rotated also. The organization operated fairly smoothly, considering our 24 hour a day operation. The maintenance personnel worked a 12-hour day and had a couple of days off after four days. There was not a lot to do when they were off except rest up for the next four days.

My truck
With a white top

"Admin"
My dog

F4 Loaded ready to go

**The Bomb
In front of
My quarters

"Home Sweet
Home"**

Fuel Storage Tank

Hit by VC Rocket

**Barracks Hit
By VC Rocket**

**5 maintenance
Men killed
38 wounded**

C-130--Hit by

VC Rocket

My job was back to 7 days a week with a little time off for flying occasionally and in the evenings, I spent a couple of hours in the lapidary shop grinding on opals. It was quite relaxing after a hard day to spend a couple of hours over there. Every time I accumulated a few polished stones, I would either send them over to Bangkok or take them over if I got a chance and have them set in the Bangkok gold. I finally ran out of my two ounce package and had someone pick up another couple of ounces for me. They were not nearly as good quality as the ones the opal merchant picked out for me.

My tour finally reached the end and my replacement came in. As I briefed him on the aspects of the job, I was sure that he was not going to do as good a job as I had. You might think that sounds conceited, but I felt that people who worked for me had been like a big family and I really was leery about turning them over to the new guy. My tour in Viet Nam had been slightly over a year.

My new assignment was to the Headquarters, Air Force Special Operations Force, which was a Major Command, although, a small one. The Headquarters was located at Eglin AFB in Florida. Eglin AFB was on the "panhandle" of Florida, near Ft. Walton Beach. I was not displeased with the assignment except for its distance from Madera, California where my parents lived. They were both getting along in years and I would have rather have been closer to them.

Chapter 25
Eglin AFB, Florida

When I knew that my tour in Viet Nam was definitely going to end (a little over a year), Tina put our house in Madera on the market. We knew that we were going to Florida and did not want to have a house in Madera to worry about. We got it sold for about what we had in it and were pleased about that. I took some leave when I returned from Viet Nam and we got everything settled in Madera and we were ready to take off for the Florida assignment. Beckie had graduated from High School in Madera while I was gone.

The movers came and loaded up all our household goods and off we went. We visited with relatives and friends along the way, taking our time. We had some leave time and the allowed travel time from California to Florida, so we did not have to hurry.

As we got to El Paso, I said that I knew a great restaurant just across the bridge and thought that we should go over there for lunch. I had not been to El Paso since we were stationed in Colorado Springs and several of us used to fly down there and go across the border for cheap booze. I thought that I knew exactly where to drive to so we could park and walk into Juarez for a great meal. I was driving toward the border and found that I was on a divided highway with no way to get off. It took us directly into Mexico. I really did not want to go into Mexico with our car and all of our luggage and our dog (the poodle that we got in Japan). After we got into Juarez, I turned around and headed back to the border, but I stopped at a booze store and bought a couple of bottles to bring back. We got to the border and the US Border Patrol officer started to question us. I guess it sounded suspicious to him when we said that we had only been in Mexico for 20 minutes. He asked us to open the trunk, which he just casually inspected and then he asked us if we had the dog's shot record. We did not have it and after a little hassle and looking at my military orders, he finally grinned and let us pass back into the US. I not only got a hassling from the border guard, but also was razzed all the way to Florida by the two female occupants of the car about my great restaurant in Mexico.

When we arrived at Eglin AFB, our furniture had not arrived yet and we lived in the base guesthouse for a couple of weeks until it arrived. The first quarters that we were assigned were not Colonel's quarters. There were none available at the time so we moved into a smaller set of quarters until Colonel's quarters became available. They were quite adequate and we had a nice back yard with lots of squirrels that became quite friendly with Beckie. They would climb all over her when she had some nuts for them. The beach was across the street from us, but not far.

I checked into my job, which was Deputy Commander for Materiel for the Air Force Special Operation Force. I was replacing a Colonel who was retiring, so we had a few days of overlap in the assumption of the new job. There were several bases that had organizations that were under the control of our Headquarters, so I had to get out to them and get familiar with their operations. I had a small, but excellent staff, who knew their jobs and could keep me out of trouble.

Since we lived near the water, I thought it would be nice if we had a boat. I saw an ad in the base bulletin for a sailboat with trailer. I called and the boat was still available so I went over and bought it. It was a small (14 foot) sailboat with a centerboard instead of a keel. I knew nothing about sailing and the officer from whom I bought the boat asked if I had ever sailed. I told him that I had not and he kindly gave me a book on sailing. That night I started reading the book and discovered that there was a lot more to sailing than I had thought. The next day I said to Beckie, "Let's go sailing." Her reply was, "Did you read that book?" I said, "Oh, I got about half way through it." She said, "What if we sail beyond the part that you read?" I smartly replied, "What I read does not sound too difficult. After all, if I can fly an airplane I should be able to handle this little sailboat." I

139

later found out that smart answers do not make up for a lack of knowledge.

Beckie and I hauled the boat and trailer across the street and onto the beach where we could launch it. Tina went along to watch this operation, but she was afraid of water and would not go out in that boat on a bet. We got the boat into the water; we had to wade out to get it into deep enough water so that we could get into the boat. The water was not very cold and the air was brisk, but not cold. It was January, but after all, we were in sunny Florida. The breeze was from the water and it was not difficult to sail away from shore at an angle. We sailed out about a third of a mile and I decided to "come about". (I had learned that nautical term from reading ½ of the book last night.) I turned the bow of the boat into the wind and the boat would not go around far enough to catch the wind on the other side of the sail. I tried several times to go through the "come about" maneuver and was unsuccessful. I decided just to go around the other way. I had not read that far, but I did not know it. Going around the other way was called jibe and the boom came over fast when the wind caught the other side of the sail and, we ducked, but with our weight and the weight of the boom on the same side of the boat, it capsized.

Although we were quite a distance from shore, we were over a sand bar and the water was only a little over waist deep. Beckie and I were standing in the water, laughing, but we were on the side of the boat away from shore and Tina could not see us. She was panicking on the beach. Fortunately, the officer I bought the boat from had mentioned the recovery from capsizing the boat. It was very simple, just put your weight on the centerboard and the boat would right itself. I did that, the sail came up out of the water, and the boat righted itself. Beckie and I climbed back in and set sail again. We were wet and chilled, but we dried off quickly and had a great day. I did learn how to "come about" before we finished sailing very far. Tina was OK and did not call the Coast Guard to rescue us when she saw the boat come upright and we climbed back in. We had a lot of fun with that boat while we were in Florida. After we moved to quarters on the beach, it was great. We just pulled it up on the beach when we were done sailing, took the sail off and put it into our carport.

After we moved into our new quarters, we were just a few doors down the beach from my boss, Brigadier General Knight. He was a great person to work for and we became quite friendly. We played golf together every Saturday. My job was a five day per week job with a few hours on Saturday and occasional at night. There was some travel involved, but not nearly as much as some of my previous jobs. It was a delight and the climate and beaches were a real pleasure. There was a small college nearby, Beckie enrolled there, and we were all happy with life in sunny Florida. Our quarters were nice and our backyard sloped down to the beach of Choctawhatchee Bay. There was a spit of land between the bay and the Gulf of Mexico. The beaches on the Gulf were like powdered sugar, very white and very fine sand. We all enjoyed going to the beaches there.

We had only been there a few weeks when the General's secretary called and said that the General wanted me and my family in his office at a certain time. Of course, we went. I was quite surprised and pleased when the General made a formal presentation of the Legion of Merit Medal (LOM) to me for my service in Viet Nam. He had the AF photographer there to take pictures of the presentation. It was a big event. The Medal had been recommended when I left Viet Nam and took some time to process and to be approved at Headquarters USAF. The LOM was a high-ranking medal and I was pleased that the boss in Viet Nam thought enough of me and my work to recommend the award.

Southern Airways airplanes flew into Eglin AFB. That was our commercial airline if we had to fly out of there commercially. Beckie met one of the flight attendants and she told her that they had a new class coming up for flight attendants. Beckie was interested; she applied for a job as Flight Attendant, and was selected for the training in Atlanta. The selection process was very rigid in those days; weight, height, appearance and attitude were all considered. We were quite proud when Beckie was selected for the training.

The training program for Flight Attendant took a couple of months and as graduation neared, the company sent us a couple of passes so we could attend the graduation exercise. The students were required to have a training flight with a supervising instructor prior to graduation. We did not know that the flight we were taking to Atlanta was Beckie's supervised flight. As we boarded the aircraft, Beckie was standing in the entryway and checking tickets. Tina walked almost completely by her and then recognized her. She said, "My God, Dick, it's Beckie." and stopped all traffic onto the airplane. Beckie's appearance had changed rather dramatically since she had left home. Part of the training was the "beauty school", the girls were taught to apply make-up properly, and Beckie's hair had been completely restyled. She was quite a different girl in appearance. Of course, we got a few hugs in while people waited to board the aircraft.

On the flight up to Atlanta, I had an aisle seat and one time, as Beckie walked by, I reached out and patted her on the fanny, just a little love pat. The supervising flight attendant held up her hands and quickly announced to all passengers, "Don't get any ideas; no one else can do that. That's her Dad." Everyone got a chuckle out of that.

At the graduation exercise, I was allowed to pin Beckie's wings onto her uniform. That was a thrill for both of us.

While we were at Eglin AFB, Rick was sent to Navy photographers' school at Pensacola, which was pretty close to Eglin, so he got over to Eglin to visit us quite a few times. He and his buddies enjoyed the sailboat and I learned a little more about sailing from them.

We enjoyed my tour at Eglin. The base golf course was super; our quarters were nice and right on the beach. If the Air Force had left me at Eglin, I would have stayed in the Air Force forever. That was not to be, however. I got word that I was being transferred to Cannon AFB at Clovis, New Mexico. There was an

F-111 wing there that was in big trouble from a maintenance standpoint and someone realized that I had experience with F-111s and had been Chief of Maintenance in several Fighter Wings. I was not too happy about the assignment, but I was a career officer and when I was told to jump, I just said, "How high."

I got a flight out to Clovis to look over the situation there. I wanted to see what the job was going to be (although I thought I knew) and I wanted to take a look at our quarters. It was in the middle of the winter when I flew out there and, after I was there for a few days and ready to go back to Florida, a nasty winter storm blew in. The weather was terrible and the T-39 that I came down in could not get to Cannon AFB to get me out. It looked like I was going to be there for a while, so I called the railroad station in Clovis to see if I could get out on a train to some place where the aircraft could get in to pick me up. I got the railroad guy on the phone and told him that I wanted to get out of there on the first train that I could get on. He said, "Mister, to get out of here on a train you have to be a cow." I got the point; there were no passenger trains out of Clovis. There were many feed yards where the cattle were fattened up before shipping them out on a train; but I was not the right type for riding the train out of Clovis. I had to wait another couple of days before an airplane could pick me up. After that escapade, Florida looked even better.

My boss said that he could probably pull some strings and get my assignment changed to Headquarters Tactical Air Command in Virginia, but I said, "Thanks, but I really feel that I can do a lot of good at Cannon." The Wing was in a bad shape, from a maintenance standpoint, and that was what all of my years of experience had trained me for -- go in and fix it. I had been exposed to the F-111s at their beginnings and was familiar with many of the problems that I was going to encounter. Therefore, our beautiful tour at Eglin AFB came to a halt and off we went to Cannon AFB. There were just the two of us at that time. Rick was still in the Navy and Beckie was flying for Southern Airways, she was domiciled in Memphis.

Chapter 26
Cannon AFB, Clovis, NM

I had looked at our quarters while I was at Cannon AFB and they were very nice. They were on a circular cul-de-sac called Crossbow Circle and all of the quarters there were for Colonels except for the one right next to ours, which was for a Brigadier General who was the Air Division Commander. I was quite pleased with our quarters, but not too pleased with the location of the base. Tina and I had decided long ago that we were going to enjoy every place that we were stationed and treat each place as a new and pleasant experience. That philosophy had made our moving around much more pleasant and our children had enjoyed our many different assignments as new and interesting places. Clovis, however, and Cannon AFB made that philosophy a little more difficult to execute. I don't mean to say that we did not enjoy our tour there, but we had many assignments that were much more enjoyable.

My job was challenging. The aircraft in-commission-rate was way below the acceptable level and it was my job to get that taken care of. The F-111 was an extremely difficult airplane to keep in commission and our parts situation was less than desirable. We had our own repair capability for many of the parts, but many of them had to be replaced with new ones or sent to an Air Force Depot for repair.

During my time there, the aircraft developed a fuel leak problem from the tanks in the aft portion of the aircraft. That portion had been built by a sub-contractor and then shipped to the General Dynamics factory where the aircraft were assembled. The company that had built the aft sections of the aircraft had used a sealant in the manufacture process that was reverting to the liquid state and allowing fuel to leak from the tanks in that portion of the aircraft.

The tanks were built, using the skin of the aircraft, and sealing all of the seams with a special sealant. The sealant was mixed just prior to its use and one portion of it was required to be kept at a very low temperature until the mix took place. If the temperature of the second part of the mixture was not controlled prior to the mix, the sealant would revert to a liquid state after a period of time. That was what we were faced with and my job was to get it fixed. We had to import special teams to go into the tanks, remove the old sealant and replace it with a properly mixed sealant. What a job! Every one of our 50 aircraft had to have that done.

There were other huge maintenance problems with the F-111 (McNamara's Dream Aircraft). One large circuit board for the computer was flexible and was folded to insert it into place. We were having failures of the computer at high altitude and finally discovered that the folded circuit board was shorting out at high altitude because of the extreme cold. We had to develop a method of testing the boards while they were folded and inside a freezer to simulate the high altitude temperatures. The on-board computer was critical to the mission of the aircraft. The complete mission was programmed into the computer on the ground and the aircraft flew at prescribed altitudes and bombed the target that was programmed unless the computer screwed up. There was a redundant system, but both could fail and then the mission could not be completed.

The aircraft was a "swing wing" aircraft. The wings swept back for high-speed operation and were moved into the forward position for low speed operation (take off and landing). There were two large pins on which the wings were mounted and there was a failure of one of those pins in one of the aircraft and the aircraft was lost. Upon inspection of the wreckage, it was discovered that the pin had crystallized and after much research it was discovered that the pin had failed due to crystallization brought about by the extreme cold of high altitude flight. A special hanger and test equipment were designed and built at McClellan AFB in California to test each aircraft for possible faulty pins. The aircraft was moved into the hanger and installed into a set of jacks that could cause the wings to flex. The hanger temperature was reduced to 40 degrees below zero and the aircraft was "cold soaked" for 24 hours. After it was cold enough, the jacks were operated and sensors all over the wings would give an indication if there were any crystallization in the large pins that held the wings on the aircraft. Several were discovered and replaced. It was a long and tedious test and each aircraft had to be flown to California to go through the test. Just imagine the refrigeration equipment that was required to bring the temperature of the hanger and the aircraft down to -40 degrees.

I was only at Cannon for a short time when I became the Deputy Commander for Material. That meant that I was not only responsible for the maintenance of the aircraft, but for the supply of all parts also. There were about 4500 people under my area of responsibility and billions of dollars worth of materials. I, in turn, was responsible to the Wing Commander. I was putting in long hours and, although I didn't work all day every day of the week, I was down around the aircraft and flight line at some time nearly every day. Cannon AFB did have a nine hole golf course and Tina and I did get to play every once in a while.

I was, in addition to my other duties, the chairman of the golf committee. We were responsible for the way that the course was used and maintained. The golf pro was the operator of the course but he reported to my committee and me. The Arabs reduced our oil supply ---- that was the big oil crunch of the 1970s. The Wing Commander was not a golfer and one of his first remarks at a staff meeting where we were discussing the oil shortage and how it would affect our mission was, "We will cut off the gasoline for the mowers at the golf course. That will save a lot of gas." I strongly objected! I did find enough gas to run the mowers for the golf course during our oil shortage.

That was the time when the maximum speed for automobiles was mandated at 55 MPH. That was the most economical speed at which to operate a car, but did it ever feel like you were crawling. Tina and I drove over to Amarillo, Texas shortly after the 55 MPH speed limit was established and we did get excellent mileage on the car, but it was so slow that we could hardly stand it. In the wide-open, flat land that we had there in that part of the country it was unbelievably slow.

Since my job no longer called for active flying, I was "excused from flying". That meant that I could no longer fly, but continued to receive my flight pay. I tossed my form 5 (a complete record of my Air force flying) onto a clerk's desk and asked him to go through it and find out how many different airplanes I had flown during my time in the Air Force. After a couple of days, he came up with 43 different types that I had flown as pilot, co-pilot, instructor pilot or command pilot. They included cargo, fighters, bombers and helicopters and speeds from 0 (hovering in a helicopter) to mach 2.1 in an F-4.

During our time there, at Cannon AFB, our son Rick finished his tour in the Navy and came home. He was much more mature and ready to go to college. The University of Eastern New Mexico was located just a few miles from Clovis and he enrolled there. He commuted from our quarters to school for a while, and then moved into the dorm where it was more convenient.

My office was located in the second floor of one of the hangers. The Wing Commander and Deputy for Operations were also located in the hanger. The offices were on a second floor, kind of a mezzanine floor. The offices were adequate and were comfortable enough most of the time. One day in January of 1974, I got to my office at about 7 AM, the heat had gone off in the hanger, and my office was a huge refrigerator. It was below freezing in the office. Later in the day, I went to staff meeting and, before the meeting started, was doodling on a pad that I had for taking notes. I was calculating the difference that I would take home in pay for continuing on active duty and that which I would take home if I retired. At that time, I had over 32 years of service for retirement purposes. The maximum retirement pay was acquired at 30 years of service, so I was not gaining anything by continuing on active duty. The Base Commander was sitting next to me and watching my calculations and he had about the same service time as I did. We were both astounded at the small difference in take home pay for active duty and retired pay. One

147

item of difference was that retired pay was not taxed for Social Security. Then, of course, since there was less pay there would be less income tax.

I said to him, "Do you realize that I am working my butt off for less than $600 per month." That was the difference between my take-home pay for active duty and for retirement pay. The freezing office was the crowning blow. I put in my retirement papers shortly after that staff meeting. I specified that I wanted to retire on the 1st day of May 1974. As the papers processed and got to the Wing Commander's office he called me and asked me if I would reconsider and extend that date another 6 months. I was pleased that he appreciated all the work that I had done and was doing to keep the aircraft flying and setting records for in-commission status for our fleet, but I had firmly decided to call it quits and retire on the 1st day of May. Tina and I had discussed it thoroughly before I had put in my papers for retirement.

The Base Commander put in his retirement papers for a couple of months later.

The officers of the Wing put on a big retirement party for me. They had prepared slides of pictures throughout my whole life from infancy onward. They were terrific and there was a very comical narrative along with them. The Officers' Club was packed. Our friend Carolyn Skaggs flew in from California for the event. She had to give a speech and was quaking in her boots. Our next-door neighbor, Brigadier General Robbie Risner, sat right beside her and that flustered her even more. The officers of my staff gave me a "roast". It was a great party.

The next day was the last day of April 1974 and there was a parade and presentation of awards. I was awarded the Air Force Meritorious Service Medal for my service at Cannon Air Force Base. It was a grand send-off. My military career had ended. I was officially retired. I was 51 years old.

Epilogue

After I retired from the Air Force in 1974, Tina and I took a year to find our place in the sun. We returned to the Fort Walton Beach area of Florida where we had been stationed at Eglin AFB. It was too hot, humid and buggy to suit us. We tried McAllen, Texas where we had purchased a grape fruit grove while we were in Clovis, New Mexico. It was too hot, humid and buggy. We drove to southern California and began our search in the San Diego area. We headed north along the coast, stopping at many places to check the real estate. We liked several areas, but when we got to Santa Barbara ---- that was it. We had found our place in the sun. We moved to Santa Barbara in 1975.

I went to work for a large company in the real estate business after I discovered that playing golf every day could become boring. Merrill Lynch bought out the company, and I stayed on with Merrill Lynch and eventually managed the downtown Santa Barbara branch for them.

In 1986 we took a trip to Tucson to visit my cousin and, before we left Santa Barbara, we were told by a friend to check out Green Valley while we were in the area. Green Valley is just south of Tucson. We checked it out, found a house we liked right on a golf course, and moved to Green Valley in 1987. We never regretted our move to Green Valley and we enjoyed our home and the Desert Hills Golf Club where we joined and played for many years.

Tina died in 2004, after a lingering illness. She is now resting in Arlington National Cemetery where I will eventually join her. I lived alone in that big house for a couple of years and then decided to move to a Garden Home in La Posada, a beautiful retirement community in Green Valley. I now reside in my garden home with my two cats, Koko and Chan.

On March 26, 2007, just after my 84th birthday, I got to

fly a B-17 again. On that date, 63 years previously, I flew a mission out of England, in a B-17, to bomb a German Rocket site near La Glacerie, France. It was my 21st mission and a pretty easy one. We had some FLAK, but no fighters. What a thrill it was to get to fly the old bird again and this time no one was shooting at me. My last flight in a B-17 had been in late 1944. I flew a couple of B-17's after I returned from England.

The plane that I got to fly is a beautifully restored B-17G. The name of the aircraft is "Liberty Bell" and it belongs to the Liberty Foundation. It is painted in the colors and markings of the 390th Bomb Group to which I was assigned in England. The man who owns the aircraft is Don Brooks and his father was a gunner in the 390th during our time in England. Don is the President of the Board of Directors of the 390th Memorial Museum Foundation, the organization that supports the 390th Memorial Museum, located on the grounds of the Pima Air and Space Museum, in Tucson, Arizona. I serve as a Docent at the Museum every Thursday and I am also on the Board of Directors for the Foundation. I had been telling Don that I did not want to ride in his beautiful airplane, but that I wanted to fly it. I finally got my chance and what a thrill it was. The airplane was in Tucson for a week while we had a reunion of the 390th Memorial Foundation. The last two days that it was here, the aircraft was available to the public for viewing and rides. The charge of $430 per person for the rides does not quite cover the expense of operating the aircraft, but it is a wonderful experience for those enthusiasts of classic WWII aircraft. After the week here, it was being ferried to the Deer Valley airport, north of Phoenix, for a week of display and rides there. I was privileged to fly it for about 25 minutes enroute to Deer Valley. What a kick that was. The airplane handled beautifully, and I kept it upright all the time I was at the controls. I had forgotten how loud the engine noise was in the B-17, but when I slid into the left seat and put the headset on, the noise was greatly reduced. The engines purred like a kitten and the airplane flew like a dream.

Since I am now revising this book, I must tell you of a

couple of recent significant happenings. In October of 2014 I was awarded the French Legion of Honor. That is France's highest award. The medal was pinned on by the French Consulate's representative and the citation was read in French – very impressive. Many of my family members were here for the presentation.

In February of 2015, I got to fly a Ford Trimotor airplane, just for a few minutes, but it was a thrill. I told the pilot that I had flown airplanes with 6 engines, 4 engines, 2 engines, 1engine and one with no engine, but I had never flown one with three engines. He let me fly it just for a few minutes in the traffic pattern. The beautiful old airplane was made in 1929. WOW

Richard Bushong

Richard retired from the United States Air Force in 1974. His retirement order states 32 years and 8 days total service. Five and a half of those years were with the Reserve Forces between wars, all the rest of that time was active duty.

During his 32 years of service, Richard Bushong flew a total of 43 different types of military aircraft. The types that he flew are:
A-20, A-24, A-25, AT-10, AT-6, AT-9, B-17, B-24, B-25, B-26, B-29, B-47, B-50, B-57, BT-13, C-121, C-123, C-45, C-47, C-50, C-54, C-64, C-82, C-84, F-4, H-13, H-21, KB-29, L-20, LC-126, P-39, P-40, P-63, PQ-14, PT-19, SA-10, T-11, T-29, T-33, T-39, T-7, U-3, UC-78

He flew at speeds varying from 0 speed (hover) in a helicopter to Mach 2.1 in the F-4 aircraft. It is noticeable that all of the aircraft that he flew are out of active service and, if any of them are still in existence, they are genuine antiques. But then, so is Richard Bushong.

Richard also flew several civilian aircraft, nine or ten different types, but who was counting? He flew, part-time, for Applied Magnetics while living in Santa Barbara. The company airplane was an executive configured Merlin.

Richard in his retirement has served on the Board of Directors and as docent for the 390th Memorial Museum, a one of a kind museum, built by the veterans of his WWII B-17 Bomb Group. The museum is located on the grounds of Pima Air and Space museum in Tucson, Arizona and displays the B-17 "Flying Fortress".

A portion of the proceeds from the sale of this book will be donated to the 390th Memorial Museum